CW01186097

RUCKSACK GUIDE

Ski mountaineering and snowshoeing

ALUN RICHARDSON British Mountain Guides

ILLUSTRATED BY GEORGE MANLEY

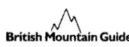

A&C BLACK • LONDON

Note
Whilst every effort has been made to ensure that the content of this book is as technically accurate and as sound as possible, neither the author nor the publishers can accept responsibility for any injury or loss sustained as a result of the use of this material.

Published by A & C Black Publishers Ltd
36 Soho Square, London W1D 3QY
www.acblack.com

Copyright © 2009 Alun Richardson

ISBN 978 0 7136 8686 9

All rights reserved. No part of this publication may be reproduced in any form or by any means – graphic, electronic or mechanical, including photocopying, recording, taping or information storage and retrieval systems – without the prior permission in writing of the publishers.

Alun Richardson has asserted his rights under the Copyright, Design and Patents Act, 1988, to be identified as the author of this work.

A CIP catalogue record for this book is available from the British Library.

Acknowledgements
Cover photograph © Alun Richardson
Inside photographs © Alun Richardson
except p. 124 J. Biggar
Illustrations by © George Manley
Designed by James Watson
Edited by Lucy Beevor

This book is produced using paper that is made from wood grown in managed, sustainable forests. It is natural, renewable and recyclable. The logging and manufacturing processes conform to the environmental regulations of the country of origin.

Typeset in 9/10pt Din-Light by Margaret Brain, UK

Printed and bound in China by C&C Offset Printing Co., Ltd.

CONTENTS

Acknowledgements	vi
Introduction	vii

How well do you need to ski? 2
A complex pastime 2

Equipment 4
Skis 4
 Nordic or cross country 4
 Alpine touring (AT) 6
 What to look for 7
Ski boots 9
Bindings 10
Snowshoes 13
 Weight and surface area 13
 Bindings 14
 Technique 14
Climbing skins 16
 Attaching skins 16
Ski crampons 18
Ski poles 19

Travelling light 20
Reducing weight 20
Equipment 21
 Shovel 21
 Avalanche probe 22
 Ice axe 22
 Crampons 22
What to wear 24
 Rucksack 24
 Clothing 24
 Harness 24

Avalanche transceivers and beacons 26
 Burial time 28
 Digital or analogue? 28
Miscellaneous items 30

Avalanches 32
The facts 32
The myths 34
Survival devices 36
 The ABS Avalanche Airbag 36
 The Black Diamond 'Avalung' 36
 Avalanche transceivers 36

Safe route finding 38
Avoiding avalanche terrain 38
Using the terrain 39
 Avoiding terrain traps 39
Assessing the avalanche potential 40
Slope aspect 42
Snowpack tests 43
 Ski pole test 44
 The 'shovel' test and 'ski' test 44
 The loaded column test 46
 Rutschblock test 46
Crossing a suspect slope 48
If you are caught in an avalanche 50

CONTENTS

Searching for a buried victim	51
During the avalanche	*51*
After the avalanche	*51*
Avalanche search phases	**52**
Primary search	*53*
Secondary search	*53*
Pinpoint search	*55*
Multiple burial search	*56*
Digging and probing	*58*
When you have no signal	*59*
After the rescue	*60*
Putting it all together	**62**
Before leaving	*62*

Finding good snow	**64**
Snow types	64
Aspect	66
Altitude	67
Angle	68
Assessing gradients from a distance	*69*

Basic skills	**70**
Carrying skis	71
Loosely tied	*71*
The high and low A-frame	*72*
The diagonal back sling	*73*

Skins and skinning	**76**
Care and usage	76
Care at a hut or tent	*76*
Preparation	*76*
Looking after skins when skiing	*77*
When a skin comes off	*77*
Balling up	78
Maintenance	79
Longer-term maintenance	*79*
Skinning technique	80
On hard snow	*82*
Using harscheisen	*83*
Using poles	*84*
Track setting when skinning	*86*
Turning on steep slopes	**90**
The downhill kick turn	*90*
Step around turn (clock turn)	*92*
The uphill kick turn	*94*
The alternative uphill kick-turn	*96*

Tactics for skiing slopes	**98**
General tactics	98
Skiing signals	*99*
Controlling speed in steep terrain	*100*
Falling on skis	*100*

CONTENTS

Skiing in crevassed terrain	**103**
Skiing roped up	**104**
Roping up when skinning	104
Descending roped-up	106
Holding a fall	106
Crevasse rescue	**108**
Response	**108**
When down a crevasse	109
Creating a rescue anchor	**110**
Ski anchors	110
Transferring the load to the anchor	113
After the load is transferred	**114**
Hoisting a victim	**116**
Simple pull	116
Two-team pull	116
Prusiking out	116
Hoisting using pulleys	118
Rescue sleds	**122**
Appendix	**126**
Off-piste skiing	**126**
Avalanche danger scales	**127**
North American avalanche danger scale	127
European avalanche danger scale	129
Index	**130**
Rucksack Guides	**134**
Other books in the series	134
Notes	**136**

ACKNOWLEDGEMENTS

The ideas in this book are the culmination of 25 years mountaineering and time spent discussing techniques with inspirational climbers, Mountain Guides and instructors, in particular Alan Dance, Dave Williams, Steve Lewis, Graeme Ettle, Bruce Goodlad, Eric PirieTrevor Massiah, Jim Beynon, Clive Hebblethwaite, John Taylor, Twid Turner, Louise Thomas and Pat Littlejohn.

Special thanks to Lesley Jones who supported me throughout; Clive Hebblethwaite who supplied some of the photographs; Adam Gent who assisted with the weather sections; Rhiannon Richardson and Molly Jones for help with text and diagrams; George Manley for his excellent illustrations; Robert Foss and Lucy Beevor from A&C Black; and the manufacturers who generously supported the photo shoots: DMM, Lyon Equipment, Mountain Equipment, Face West, Select Solar, Mammut and Fritschi.

Any of the opinions expressed in this book are mine alone and should not be associated with any of the above people, companies or organisations.

INTRODUCTION

Ski Mountaineering and Snowshoeing is the fifth book in the **Rucksack Guide** series and covers the skills required to become a competent ski mountaineer. This handy book can be kept in your rucksack and will help you to gain the experience to ski mountaineer safely anywhere in the world. It does not cover the technical aspects of navigation, alpinism, snow and ice climbing (see **Rucksack Guides** to *Mountain Walking and Trekking*, *Alpinism* and *Winter Mountaineering*).

The **Rucksack Guide** series tells you *what* to do in a situation, but it does not always explain *why*. If you want more information behind the decisions in these books, go to *Mountaineering: The Essential Skills for Mountaineers and Climbers* by Alun Richardson (A&C Black, 2008).

For more information about the author, his photographs and the courses he runs go to:

www.freedomphotographs.co.uk or
www.alunrichardson.co.uk.

Andy Perkins (IFMGA), Chamonix

A COMPLEX PASTIME

'Skiing is the pleasurable part of alpinism – way more pleasurable and fun than alpine climbing.'
– Michael Kennedy, former Editor of *Climbing* magazine

For the ski mountaineer, leaving a tent or a hut as the Sun creeps up over the mountains, with the prospect of a four-hour ascent and a one-hour ski back down untracked snow is the stuff of dreams. It is the most wonderful way to get away from the crowded pistes and experience the mountains in their winter clothes.

Ski mountaineering is a complex pastime combining the skills of Alpinism and skiing. You must have the ability to ski off-piste; navigate; choose a safe line; be aware of the mountain environment in winter; assess and test snow conditions for avalanches; use an avalanche transceiver, probe and shovel; travel safely on glaciers; and use the rope, ice axe and crampons for descending and ascending steep snow slopes.

Ask a Mountain Guide whom would they would rather take ski mountaineering out of a skier or a mountaineer, and they will always say the skier. Ski mountaineering is not for novice skiers, but you don't have to be an expert either. If you can combine mountaineering skills with the ability to link controlled, parallel carved turns, on-piste while wearing a small rucksack, you can probably attempt some very easy tours in good snow conditions. However, do not overestimate your skiing ability with more serious tours.

For most skiers contemplating ski mountaineering the problem is that the snow off-piste can vary from deep powder to crust. Mountaineering experience will not compensate for lack of skiing ability but, as long as you can traverse, side-slip, snowplough turn and perform a downhill kick-turn, you will be able to find your way down most slopes, albeit more slowly and, therefore, having less fun. The opposite is also true; good skiers should also be aware that losing a ski or fracturing a limb in a remote area is serious.

Skier Owen Cox

SKIS

Ski mountaineering differs from alpine skiing, in that the bindings free the heel for walking along and up snow slopes. Equipment specifically designed for ski mountaineering is always a compromise between the two disciplines of skiing and mountaineering. For instance, ski mountaineering bindings do not have all the release possibilities of the best downhill bindings; boots are lighter but, more flexible than piste boots; and ice axes are light, but do not perform very well on ice. However, the gap in safety and performance is becoming smaller.

There are two ski disciplines, each with its own band of faithful followers.

NORDIC OR CROSS COUNTRY

Nordic ski bindings leave your heels free all of the time, so you don't have to change between uphill and downhill modes. The boots flex at the toe for more natural walking and the bindings have a spring-loaded cable that fits around the heel of the boot and a front toe binding.

Nordic skiing is sometimes referred to as 'telemark' skiing, but the telemark is actually a turn, not a ski. There is no doubt that Nordic skis have an advantage on gently rolling terrain, but, unless you are an advanced Nordic skier who has mastered the telemark turn with a rucksack on, do not consider using Nordic skis for tours that have substantial steep descents, especially if you want to have fun.

A further downside of using Nordic skiing for ski mountaineering is that the boots are difficult to use with crampons and useless for kicking steps into snow.

SKIS   5

EQUIPMENT

There is a saying that goes 'free the heel and free the mind', but mine is 'fix the heel and fix the problem'.

SKIS

ALPINE TOURING (AT)

For ski tours with steep downhill sections, there is no doubt that AT gear is a superior choice and will allow an average skier to cope with a wider variety of snow conditions.

Every ski has its pros and cons and your choice will depend on the type of ski touring you do, how heavy you are and how aggressively you ski (stiffer skis need to be bent). The first thing to decide is whether travelling between huts is a priority, or making better and safer turns is more important. If it is the former, buy a lighter purpose-built touring ski that may have holes in the tips for clipping in a krab. If you are a skier at heart your task is more difficult. Modern 'All mountain' skis, such as the Salomon X-Wing Fury, are designed to be skied shorter for a given weight and height. Choose a ski between your own height to 10cm shorter, but make sure it is compatible with the combined weight of you and your rucksack.

WHERE DID IT ALL START?

Ski is an old Norse word meaning 'stick of wood'. The earliest reference to skis are on 5000-year-old drawings in Norway, but the Englishman Cecil Slingsby was one of the first Europeans to use skis for mountaineering when he crossed the 1550m Keiser Pass, Norway, in 1880. In 1888 the Norwegian Fridtjof Nansen made the first crossing of Greenland. However, the 'father' of the sport is generally regarded as the German Wilhelm von Arlt, who made the first ski ascent of the Rauris Sonnblick (3103m) in 1894. The first ski tour in the European Alps occurred in 1894 near Davos, when Sir Arthur Conan Doyle and the Branger brothers travelled from Frauenkirch to Arosa.

WAXING SKIS

It is probably not a good idea to hot wax skis before ski mountaineering, as the wax will reduce the effectiveness of the glue on the skins.

WHAT TO LOOK FOR IN A SKI

Tip width
- The wider it is compared to the waist width, the greater the pull of the ski in the turn.

Waist width
- The narrower it is, the quicker the edge change and the better the edge grip on hard snow.
- The wider it is, the more speed and tracking stability you get on off-piste snow, but the poorer the edge grip on hard snow.

Tail width
- The wider it is in relation to the waist width, the greater the guidance at the end of the turn and the support in tight turns.
- The narrower it is, the more easily the ski can slide.

Radius
- The smaller the radius, the tighter the carved turns can be.
- The larger the radius, the wider the turns.

Surface area
The bigger it is:

- the more lift the ski has in deep and soft snow; and
- the more speed stability it has on off-piste terrain.

SKIS

Flexibility
- A more flexible ski performs better in soft snow, and is more forgiving in varied conditions.
- A stiffer ski holds an edge and carves better on wind-blown, hard-packed or icy snow.
- The lighter you are the more flexible they must be, but you must also consider the torsional rigidity.

Torsional rigidity (the ability to resist twisting)
- On deep, soft or variable snow, the more tortional rigidity the better the ski holds a turn without flailing.

Colour
- Bright colours are easier to find – think of yourself in an avalanche or after a fall in deep snow.

Weight of ski and binding
- A lightweight ski makes carrying them and also skinning easier, but this must be balanced against skiing performance.

Fig. 1 *Skis come in a wide variety of types and designs – choose the one that suits your skiing style.*

SKI BOOTS

Normal ski boots can be used for simple day tours, but they are uncomfortable when used for long walks and may let snow in when loosened for walking. Purpose-built ski mountaineering boots are a compromise. They weigh less, are more flexible and have a Vibram sole for walking, can be used for kicking steps in snow and are compatible with crampons.

Ultra lightweight models have obvious advantages, but for an average skier a sturdier version will hold the feet more firmly on descents.

A good fit is important, and it is worth having your inner boot and outer shell customised to your feet (Scarpa are broader, Garmont narrower).

Fig. 2 Purpose-built ski mountaineering boots are a cross between a plastic mountaineering boot and a ski boot.

An AT binding has two positions:

1 Hinged for walking
2 Fixed for skiing

Modern AT bindings are almost as safe as standard ski bindings when used properly, but no AT binding has the safety release of the latest alpine bindings. Because the consequences of injury are more serious, start with a low setting and increase it by small increments if you find that you pre-release too often. Use ski brakes rather than safety straps; if you fall it is best not to have a ski flailing around your head.

Leading AT bindings include the Fritschi Explore and Fritschi Freeride (Fig. 3). The latter is a good choice for heavier, more aggressive skiers. The Dynafit Tourlite bindings (Fig. 4) are the lightest and strongest bindings available, but having such a small binding takes some getting used to, and you must use boots that are compatible with them.

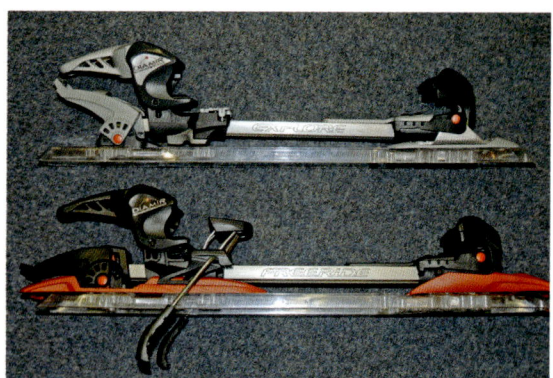

***Fig. 3** Fritschi AT bindings*

BINDINGS 11

Fig. 4 *Dynafit Tourlite bindings*

BINDINGS

The binding best-suited to approaching climbs in mountaineering boots is the Silvretta 500 model. The wire toe bail accepts standard plastic mountaineering boots without risk of damage to the lip of the boot. To prevent injury, keep your heels free, even when skiing downhill, because mountaineering boots will not release reliably when locked down.

Some specialist skis, such as Karhu Karva and Meta, have an integrated climbing skin embedded into the base and full metal edges. Their universal binding allows you to use any winter boots and the skis' wide footprint and short length make them great for first-time skiers accessing climbs.

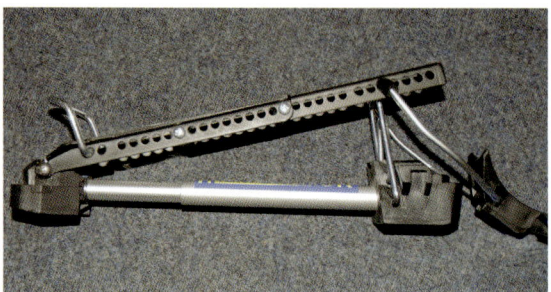

Fig. 5 *It is possible to have a taste of ski mountaineering using standard bindings with a removable insert that allow you to walk, but they are very heavy, stiff and uncomfortable on uphill sections and long traverses.*

SNOWSHOES

Snowshoes are lightweight, compact, and provide the easiest form of snow travel. Less-skilled skiers may prefer the convenience of snowshoes in crust or variable snow and when carrying a heavy pack, although they are slower overall and are not as much fun on downhill sections and in deep snow.

Snowshoes have distinct advantages for climbers unable to ski. They help:

- to avoid difficulties in deep snow;
- when approaching or retreating from ice and alpine climbs;
- when ascending or descending non-technical mountaineering routes; and
- for narrow, steep winter approaches that are difficult to ski and have lots of tight turns, trees and vegetation.

When choosing snowshoes, remember that all properly designed snowshoes work – it's just that some work better in certain conditions than others. For example, a larger snowshoe will float on loose snow more easily than a small one, but is heavier and less manoeuvrable.

WEIGHT AND SURFACE AREA

Your combined body and rucksack weight plus the type of snow will determine the size of the snowshoe needed. A common formula is for every 0.45kg of body weight, there should be 6.5 sq cm of snowshoe surface per snowshoe. Use a smaller snowshoe for climbing and mountaineering, because of the increased manoeuvrability and traction.

BINDINGS

Modern snowshoes have technical bindings and crampons for difficult terrain. Look for steel crampons that rotate on a door-type hinge; vertically orientated metal traction blades that run the length of the snowshoe's underside; and a binding that is fiddle-free, fits well and stays on all day without adjustment.

Neoprene straps are easy to grab and pull with mittens on. Nylon webbing bindings are more time consuming to adjust over large double boots, and the nylon often absorbs water and freezes.

Fig. 6 *Snowshoes*

TECHNIQUE

Snowshoe technique is much the same as walking in crampons and skis (Fig. 7).

- Lift your feet higher than normal.
- To avoid the unnatural and tiring 'straddle-gait', roll your feet slightly and slide the overlapping inner edges over each other.
- It is difficult to go backwards wearing snowshoes!

SNOWSHOES

- Don't step on the snowshoes, and don't place them over a gap, as they may break. Instead, step on top of rocks or logs.
- When jumping across streams keep snowshoes low so that the heels do not land first.
- On a steep descent soft, unconsolidated snow gives more control.
- If you must descend a steep icy section, be prepared to sidestep, making sure to plant each step firmly using 'flat foot' technique, just as you would when walking with crampons.
- If the terrain is such that a slip or fall could cause serious injury or death, remove your snowshoes, put on your crampons and get out your ice axe.

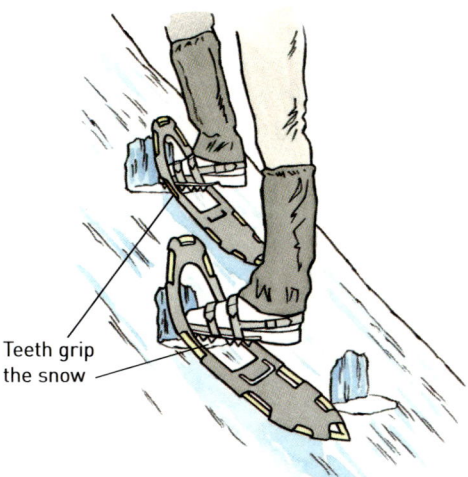

Teeth grip the snow

Fig. 7 Snowshoe technique. On very steep slopes it is still beneficial to kick the toes of the boots into the snow or use skiing/crampon techniques. Walk uphill with the snowshoes spread outward at an angle (pied en canard or duck-walking), and sidestep, contour or zigzag steep slopes.

CLIMBING SKINS

Climbing skins are temporarily glued to the ski base, which allows them to glide forwards, but not backwards. They are made from nylon or mohair fibres or a mixture of both, and vary in width and length. Nylon is cheaper and lasts longer, but mohair glides better (this difference is marked at cold temperatures).

The amount of grip a skin has depends on the length of the fibres, rather than the material it is made from – the longer the fibres, the more grip. However, given that mixed skins last three to four times longer, they may be the best compromise. If ultimately speed and glide are important, use mohair.

ATTACHING SKINS

Skins can be full length and hooked on to the back of the ski (a notch in the tail is useful), or they can be cut 15cm shorter than the length of the ski (the rear of the ski plays little part in the skinning process). The full-length system is heavier and produces more drag, but the skin may stay on the ski more effectively. If you are cutting your skins shorter make sure that you round off the ends to stop them lifting off. The best system for attaching the skin to the front of the ski is the traditional metal bracket.

Skins should not cover the ski edges (old narrow skins do not work well on modern broad skis – see p.79 for a tip on using narrow skins as spares), particularly in the centre of the ski, where it is needed to grip snow on steep slopes. Parabolic skis can have skins shaped to fit (Coll Tex) or you can buy wide, straight skins to cut to shape. After cutting, fold them in half and re-cut them so that they are perfectly symmetrical tip-to-tail and there is no glue showing; they are then easier to store. Most modern skins come with plastic sheets attached to the skin, which make it much easier to peel them apart.

CLIMBING SKINS   17

Fig. 8 *Climbing skins are glued to the base of the ski, allowing it to glide forwards, but not slide backwards on ascents (skier Lorenz Frutiger, Greenland).*

SKI CRAMPONS

Ski crampons (sometimes called *harscheisen*, German; *couteau*, French; or *ramponi*, Italian) are attached when the snow is hard and your skins are not gripping. They fit between the boot and the plate of the binding and must be compatible with your bindings.

They allow a row of metal teeth to protrude downwards on either side of the ski. When the foot and the plate of the binding are raised, the ski can glide forward; when the foot is lowered, the teeth bite into the snow.

If you are flexible enough, the new Diamir Explore binding and the Dynafits let you fix crampons without removing your boots from the skis.

Fig. 9 *Harscheisen*

SKI POLES

Telescopic poles have a tendency to collapse when you don't want them to, and the locking mechanism can jam, leading to them breaking. Therefore, use non-collapsible poles for most tours unless you need to leave your skis behind and climb to the top of the mountain on foot, carrying your poles. Look for models with padding below the handles to allow you to grip the pole lower down on traverses (you can add this yourself).

Fig. 10 Graeme Ettle IFMGA Guide

REDUCING WEIGHT

Skiing with a lightweight rucksack is more fun, uses less energy and is safer. You can use most of your usual alpine gear, but reduce the weight of every item.

- Use lightweight waterproofs.
- Divide food into individual portions.
- Take sample-sized or half-full tubes of toothpaste and sunscreen.
- Use lithium batteries for electronic devices (note: except transceivers, see p.26) so that you don't need spares.
- Avoid doubling up on personal and group equipment.
- If something can serve two purposes, use it for both rather than carry two items e.g. spare sunglasses versus goggles.
- Seal your maps and leave the map case behind.

The amount of equipment carried will also dictate the type of tour, because with heavier rucksacks and tents you are unlikely to choose steep descents. You may even resort to Nordic skis and towing a sledge.

Fig. 10 *Charlie Sommerfield travelling light*

EQUIPMENT

SHOVEL

Buy a sturdy, brightly coloured, metal shovel, with a handle that will not break when digging in hard-packed avalanche debris. You may find it easier to keep the extendable handle retracted when digging – and it is better to assume a kneeling position to avoid back injury anyway.

Fig. 11 Lorenz Frutiger digging in Greenland after a storm. Inset: a variety of snow shovels.

AVALANCHE PROBE

Avalanche probes are lightweight, sectional probes used for locating avalanche victims. The sections are connected by a wire or cord and assemble quickly to form a 2.4–3.2m probe, with a hardened tip to easily penetrate avalanche debris. Tent poles do not work!

Adjustable ski poles can be joined to form a probe, but it takes time to remove the baskets and assemble them. The resulting probe does not penetrate well and is typically only 2m long. A good compromise is for everyone in the team to carry probe-convertible ski poles, and a couple of sectional probes in the group gear.

A shovel with the avalanche probe or snow saw inside the handle is a useful innovation. However, the probe is usually too thin for adequate rigidity and too short (1.8m) for locating deep burials. A snow saw is a much better item to store in a shovel handle, as it is useful for a number of tasks, such as cutting snow blocks for igloos and wind barriers, and for rutschblocks or snow columns when testing avalanche stability.

ICE AXE

Specialist ski mountaineering models weigh about 230g and have light alloy heads. They are useful if you do not need to use them on ice, but otherwise consider a lightweight axe with a sturdier head.

CRAMPONS

Specialist lightweight, aluminium alloy crampons are suitable for most ski tours, but they are not designed for use on ice or rock and are not suitable as a general mountaineering crampon. A more robust pair is preferable for more technical tours.

EQUIPMENT

Fig. 12 Take care with avalanche probes as they are easily bent (Andy Perkins, IFMGA Guide).

WHAT TO WEAR

TRAVELLING LIGHT

RUCKSACK
Skiing with a lightweight rucksack is more fun, uses less energy and is safer. A heavy rucksack will simply accentuate any shoulder rotation, increase your chances of twisting something in a fall and make it strenuous to get back up.

For day tours, 30 litres is enough, but 50 litres may be required for more serious tours. Look for good ski attachments and try it on when it is loaded, making sure it has minimal side-to-side movement.

CLOTHING
Kit-up just like any other remote mountain venture.

- Use layers and try to keep yourself dry during and after exercise.
- Cut as much weight as you can from your upper body layers, but carry a lightweight duvet jacket, such as the Mountain Equipment Trango, or an extra fleece, in case of an emergency or bad weather.
- Use lightweight, breathable waterproofs, as normal ski clothing is too warm and is not usually flexible enough.
- The rest of your clothes should be the same as you use in the Alps for summer mountaineering.

HARNESS
A harness is vital unless you are sure that there are no crevasses or there is no need for abseiling on your tour. To save weight, you can improvise a harness from slings, but this is uncomfortable, especially when you are down a crevasse. Compromise by using a simple lightweight adjustable mountaineering harness, with a chest harness made from a sling if you are carrying a heavy rucksack.

WHAT TO WEAR

***Fig. 13** Wear the same clothing as you would to go mountaineering (skier Nigel Offley).*

CREVASSE RESCUE KIT

Carry the same rescue kit as for summer alpinism, but have two 30m x 8mm dynamic ropes to share the load (such as the randonee). Some ski mountaineers carry 8mm Dyneema cord, but a full 50m rope may be required for abseils on some tours.

TRAVELLING LIGHT

AVALANCHE TRANSCEIVERS AND BEACONS

Avalanche transceivers are worn on the body and emit a radio signal. If someone is buried in an avalanche, other transceivers can be used to pick up the signal. The receiving beacon changes the signal into a visual or audible display, which quickly guides the searcher towards the transmitting beacon.

- All modern transceivers operate on 457kHz and are compatible with one another.
- Models operating on only 2.275kHz and dual frequency models should be retired.
- Transceivers should only be used with high quality alkaline batteries, and not rechargeable lithium batteries, as their performance degrades rapidly at low charge.
- Mobile phones can interfere with the signal so switch them off.

There are two types of transceiver, and both emit signals that can be detected by each type:

1 **Digital transceivers** light up or show direction on a display panel.
2 **Analogue transceivers** respond by emitting audible beeps that get louder as they get closer to the buried transceiver. Some models also have a visual indicator (visual indicators are useful, because it is often difficult to detect changes in sound volume when there is high wind or when more than one transceiver is buried).

In transmit mode, a transceiver creates an elliptical electromagnetic field. If a second device is set to search mode it will detect this field, if it is in range. The operational range is usually around 50m for analogue and a little less for digital.

AVALANCHE TRANSCEIVERS AND BEACONS

***Fig. 14** The Pulse Barryvox transceiver. Wear an avalanche transceiver at all times, and know how to use it.*

Range is, however, completely dependent on the orientation of the transmitting transceiver to the receiving transceiver. The maximum signal is obtained when the two antennae are parallel. The antennae are usually situated on the longest side of the transceiver. Conversely, the signal is weakest when the two devices are at right angles. By moving the transceiver through an arc, a searcher can pick up the strongest signal and follow this directly to the victim. This is easiest with digital devices that give a visual indication of signal strength and the approximate distance to the victim.

BURIAL TIME
The burial time is dependant not only on the time to locate a victim, but also how long it takes to dig them out, therefore all search devices are only effective when shovels and probes are carried.

> ### RECCO OR SIMILAR PASSIVE SYSTEMS
> Passive tags are designed to perform a similar function to transceivers. However, you need specialist bulky equipment to search for one, which few ski resorts keep and no one carries off-piste. They are of questionable value.

DIGITAL OR ANALOGUE?
A digital unit is easier to learn to use, especially with a single burial. However, digital receivers are less effective with multiple burials, as the task of separating and identifying the different signals becomes much more difficult with a digital read-out than with an audible signal. Some versions allow the signal from an identified transceiver to be masked so that it does not interfere with subsequent searches.

Many professionals trained in the use of avalanche transceivers prefer an analogue model, because human ears are pretty good at differentiating between the relative strength of several signals and picking out the loudest. For the recreational user, who cannot invest a lot of time learning to use a transceiver, the digital, dual antenna technology is a better choice, because the slight lack of range is compensated by the increased search speed.

AVALANCHE TRANSCEIVERS AND BEACONS

Fig. 15 The excellent Tracker avalanche transceiver

AVALANCHE SURVIVAL FACTS

- Of skiers completely buried by an avalanche only 40 per cent survive.
- In recent years, 1347 skiers survived partial or complete burial:
  - 39 per cent dug themselves out
  - 34 per cent were dug out by friends
  - 27 per cent were recovered by rescue services mostly close to ski resorts.

MISCELLANEOUS ITEMS

You will also need the following items:

- Altimeter – essential for navigating while descending quickly
- Small LED headlamp, spare batteries and bulb
- Map and compass
- Global Positioning System (GPS). This is not a substitute for navigation skills.
- Goggles and sunglasses
- Sunscreen and lip balm
- Food
- Water. Hydration bladders freeze up. A flask is useful – pack snow into a mug and melt it with the hot water.
- Velcro ski strap – useful for tying skis together on your rucksack

Other optional items include:

- **Mobile phones and radios** Useful in emergencies, but in mountain valleys you may not receive a signal. Phones are easily damaged in a fall, are expensive and difficult to use for 'intercom' talk. New satellite phone technology may change this, but currently the expense and weight count against their use.
- **Two-way radios** Allow you to direct the group in another direction when avalanche terrain and poor visibility are combined. Rig them up with a microphone that is clipped to your jacket or rucksack strap, so you don't have to dig around for it.
- **Repair and emergency kit** (see box opposite) A smoke flare is the best way to show a pilot the wind direction. In very remote areas an Electronic Position Indicating Beacon (EPIRB) or Personal Location Beacon (PLB) is recommended.

MISCELLANEOUS ITEMS

REPAIR KIT

- Multipurpose tool
- Small amount of malleable wire
- Cable ties
- Spare pole basket
- Small hose clamps for pole repair
- Small sharpening stone
- Optional spare skin
- Optional knee brace
- If it doesn't move and it should, use WD40.
- If it moves and it shouldn't, use duct tape.
- Glues
- Coll Tex skin glue

Fig. 16 Carry a repair kit – you never know when it will be needed.

AVALANCHES

There are three things to consider:

1. If you feel uncomfortable about the level of risk, go home.
2. A great downhill run often produces a feeling of euphoria that can cloud your judgement during and after the run.
3. Get caught in an avalanche and your chances of survival are slim.

Know and understand the following before heading into the mountains:

- Ski mountaineers are in greater danger than walkers, because the cutting action of skis readily releases unstable snow.
- Many avalanche accidents occur just after new snowfall, but clear skies, little or no snowfall and light winds do not mean the avalanche danger is low.
- The victim or members of the victim's party trigger most avalanches.
- Seventy per cent of avalanches start on 30–40 degree, often convex, slopes, with exposed rocks that cause stress concentrations, and often near the crest of a ridge. Most red runs average 20 degrees and black runs are seldom steeper than 35 degrees, although on both there may be steeper sections. Carry an inclinometer or measure the angle using ski poles (see p. 68).
- Only 6 per cent of avalanches happen on slopes of less than 25 degrees and they are usually wet snow avalanches. They travel slowly, but often over considerable distances with great force and usually set solid.

THE FACTS

- Almost all victims survive if they are not seriously injured, not buried deeper than 2m and found within 18 minutes. US research indicates that the survival rate of victims buried 2m or deeper is only 4 per cent.
- After 18 minutes, survival declines rapidly, and after 35 minutes only victims that have a good air pocket survive. It is therefore crucial that the victim is located and dug out as quickly as possible.
- In perfect conditions, finding someone with an avalanche transceiver and probe takes 3–5 minutes and digging to a depth of 1m with a shovel takes 10–15 minutes.

Fig. 17 Even small avalanches can result in a lot of snow at the base of the slide.

THE MYTHS

- **'Avalanches can be triggered by shouting.'**
  Avalanches cannot be triggered by most sounds, because any forces exerted in sound waves are far too low. The very large shockwaves produced by explosions can trigger avalanches, however, if they are close enough to the surface.

- **'Avalanches strike without warning.'**
  Avalanches usually give obvious signs. The process of creating avalanche conditions begins many hours – or even days – before.

- **'If you make it across a suspect slope without it avalanching, it is safe.'**
  All that it tells you is that you did not load it enough to release an avalanche.

- **'Avalanches only happen during storms.'**
  Storms only bring the snow; what happens in the snowpack to create avalanche conditions depends on many factors.

- **'Waiting 2-3 days after storms is safe.'**
  Avalanche conditions can occur whenever there is a slope and snow. Wind can create avalanche conditions on an otherwise sunny day by redistributing snow.

- **'If there are tracks then the slope is safe.'**
  This may be, but it may also be because the previous climbers did not load the slope enough to trigger an avalanche.

- **'The slope has never been known to slide, so it's safe.'**
  Unless its less than 25 degrees, the slope has the potential to avalanche.

- **'Transceivers keep you safe.'**
  All transceivers do is enable your rescuers to locate you – whether you are alive is another matter.

- **'There is not enough snow to avalanche.'**
  Snow can slide on any surface and early season full-depth avalanches are common.

Nearly all avalanche terrain can be avoided (Col des Ecandies, The High Level Route, Chamonix to Zermatt).

SURVIVAL DEVICES

If you are caught in an avalanche your chances of survival are greatly enhanced if you are:

- Close to the surface
- You can create an air space to breathe
- You can be located quickly.

Several devices have been developed to increase your survival chances if you are caught in an avalanche. The danger is that they may give you a false sense of security.

THE ABS AVALANCHE AIRBAG
Mortality of completely buried victims is extremely high, and a partially buried victim is more likely to be located quickly. The ABS Avalanche Airbag lowers the risk of complete burial. It is a rucksack with two plastic balloons built into it – when a cord is pulled, these inflate in seconds and help keep you on the top of the avalanche. It is only feasible for use by off-piste skiers and ski mountaineers doing short day tours.

THE BLACK DIAMOND 'AVALUNG'
Creating an air pocket in front of your mouth and nose can prolong survival. However, of those that die it is due to the increased levels of CO_2. The 'Avalung' safety vest (Fig. 18) removes exhaled air and vents it behind the victim. There is as yet no statistical evidence to show its use increases survival, but tests have shown that a completely buried person can survive for up to an hour using the 'Avalung'.

AVALANCHE TRANSCEIVERS
Transceivers increase your chances of survival by helping others to locate you quickly.

SURVIVAL DEVICES

Fig. 18 The Black Diamond 'Avalung'

PRACTICE USING YOUR TRANSCEIVER

- Real avalanches happen during bad weather, which limits visibility and group communications. Practising only on calm sunny days, gives you a false notion of your skills.
- Real avalanches happen when you are tired, cold, hungry and dehydrated. Often it is the very presence of one or more of these human factors that caused you to get caught in the first place.
- In a real search there is often shock, disorganisation, disagreement and panic.
- As soon as avalanches come to a stop they set like concrete, making it difficult to dig and also reducing the transceiver signal range.

AVOIDING AVALANCHE TERRAIN

'Europeans may lead the world in transceiver technology and guide training, but they also lead the world in avalanche and climbing accidents and fatalities.'
– David Spring, Ski Patrol Rescue Team (SPART), WA, USA

Nearly all avalanche terrain can be avoided. The process starts at home (read guidebooks and maps to find the safest route and see *Rucksack Guide: Winter Mountaineering*, 2009) and continues when you leave your car, hut or tent, and throughout the day, both on the ascent and the descent.

When planning your tour you could set absolute limits depending on the snow conditions. When the conditions are potentially dangerous, follow gentle slopes without steep ground above them:

- 30 degrees in NW-, N-, NE-facing slopes when the danger is moderate
- 30 degrees on all slopes when the danger is considerable
- 25 degrees or less when the danger is high.

When planning your route, you can deduce the slope angle from the separation of the contour lines on the map – use 1:25,000 maps for greater accuracy. The French Alps have a 10m vertical interval, which changes to 20m when you cross into Switzerland. However, maps do not show all the bumps and hollows and there might be steeper sections.

For 20m vertical intervals between contours (Swiss maps), convert slope gradients as follows:

SWISS MAP CONVERSION

Gradient	Scale 1:25,000	Scale 1:50,000
15 degrees	3.0mm	1.5mm
20 degrees	2.2mm	1.1mm
30 degrees	1.4mm	0.7mm
45 degrees	0.8mm	0.4mm

USING THE TERRAIN

When the conditions are dangerous, you can use the terrain to help you find a safe route. Densely packed, mature trees may increase the stability of the slope and provide some protection from a slide. Think about which side of the valley to ascend according to the Sun's direction, the temperature and where the avalanches are most likely to fall. Try to use high points such as ridges, knolls, or the tops of small hills, and wide valleys to travel along.

AVOIDING TERRAIN TRAPS
There are a number of terrain traps to avoid:

- **Drop offs** Even a small slide could be severe if it carries you over a cliff or on to rocks.
- **V-shaped valleys or gullies** The snow from a slide is forced into a confined area and could bury you to a great depth.
- **Old moraine areas** You could sustain damage sliding over the rocks and boulders. Be wary of avalanche cone slopes: it means that avalanches fall there regularly.
- **Convex slopes** They are more hazardous, because the point of maximum convexity is a frequent site of tension fracture.
- **Ridge crests** Avalanches are more likely to be triggered where the depth of the weak layers of snow is shallow (50cm or less below the surface) such as near ridge crests or at the edges of gulleys and hollows.

ASSESSING THE AVALANCHE POTENTIAL

Get an avalanche bulletin and a weather forecast. Consider the following:

WHAT TO ASSESS	
Ask:	**Think:**
Can you see fresh avalanches?	On which slopes and in which orientation?
Is it the first good day after heavy snow?	Loading*
Was it very cold when the snow started falling?	Potential icy layer under new snow
Does the snow settle under your skis or make a 'wumph' sound?	Potential slab avalanche
Is snow breaking up and sliding away at turns?	Potential slab avalanche
Are there cracks in the snow?	Potential pack moving
Is there a lot of new snow on trees?	Loading
Is a lot of snow still falling?	Loading
Can you see to assess the steepness of the slope?	70% of avalanches occur at a steepness of 30 degrees or more
Is it a lee slope?	Potential slab avalanche
Is it a convex slope?	Stress at the top of the slope
Are you close to ridge crest?	Small slab on the leeside
Can you see fresh snow ripples, rime or sastrugi?	In what direction is the wind blowing?
Is the wind strong?	Where are the lee slopes?
Can you see plumes of spindrift (sprays of snow blown by the wind)?	In what direction is the snow blowing?
Has there been a sudden rise in temperature?	Potential pack instability and cornice collapse

***Loading** A lot of fresh snow adds extra weight to the snowpack, which causes loading. If a weak layer exists, it could slide.

Skinning in Otzal, Alps, Austria

SLOPE ASPECT

The aspect of a slope affects the temperature of the snowpack. A cold snowpack tends to develop more persistent weak-layers, such as facets and surface hoar (frost). Therefore the majority of avalanche accidents occur on colder north- and east-facing slopes.

In warm, wet snow conditions, the opposite occurs and south- and west-facing slopes produce more wet avalanches than the more shady slopes. However, during prolonged cloudy or stormy conditions, when the Sun seldom shines on the snow, there will be very little difference between sunny and shady slopes.

If you are skiing in the Southern Hemisphere, the opposite occurs (south-facing slopes are colder than those facing north).

Fig. 19 *Skiing in Chamonix (skier Charlie Sommerfield)*

SNOWPACK TESTS

You should have built up a picture of the snow's probable stability from the avalanche report, the prevailing weather and as you travel, but there are times when you must assess the risk of skiing a particular slope.

Assessing a slope's stability is a complex issue, and even after assessment you may not know whether it is safe or not to travel on. If the slope is greater than 25 degrees with new snow it is always going to be a risk. If you have any doubts, do not ski – whatever the following tests tell you.

The problem with the observations gained from snowpack tests is that they only provide partial information about existing avalanche conditions. You must mix the information they provide with what has been happening beforehand in order to make a reasonable evaluation of the current hazards and risk factor.

If you find a weak layer you must also consider the strength and quantity of snow on top of it:

- Is the air temperature cold or warm?
- When did the last snowfall take place?
- Have you seen any avalanches down to the weak layer found in your pit?
- Is the snow above the weak layer loose or bonded together to form a slab?
- How far down is the weak layer (avalanches are rarely triggered when it is greater than 1.5m deep)?

It is important to practice snowpack tests so that you can match previous and current observations. Dig your pit and test in the most representative spot on the slope you want to ski. If you release something on a 30-degree slope it will release more easily on a 40-degree slope!

SKI POLE TEST

Push your pole into the snow at a consistent rate and feel for changes in resistance as you encounter layers. This should never be used as the sole judge of stability, but more as an indication that snow conditions have changed and further testing is required. The main advantage is that it is quick.

THE 'SHOVEL' TEST AND 'SKI' TEST

The shovel test (Fig. 20) judges the cohesiveness of the layers. It must be practiced over many years, to the point where you build up a feeling for the stability of layers (most beginners tend to overrate the danger).

One potential problem of this test is that you are removing the weight of snow from the layer each time you dig and it is difficult to assess the influence of this factor. Because of the small sample size, you need to do several tests to get a true feel for the stability of the snow.

- Having made the snow pit observations, isolate a wedge-shaped block, cutting down to the top of the next identified layer.
- Cut behind the column to below a suspect layer (do not cut the whole column).
- Insert the shovel behind and pull straight out; don't lever on the shovel. Do this for each suspect layer.
- Look for smooth, straight shears that pop out easily. Try to rank them as easy, moderate, hard, and so on.
- If a block slides off during cutting, there is obviously a weak layer.
- If the block slides off with pressure from the shovel – and it must be a clean, smooth shear to mean anything – and there is 15cm or more snow on top, turn each block upside down to see which weak layer was involved.

SNOWPACK TESTS

An adaption of the shovel test is to isolate the column completely, insert a ski behind and pull on the ski. Some people feel it gives a better result. Whichever test you use, repeating it many times will improve your ability to assess the slope.

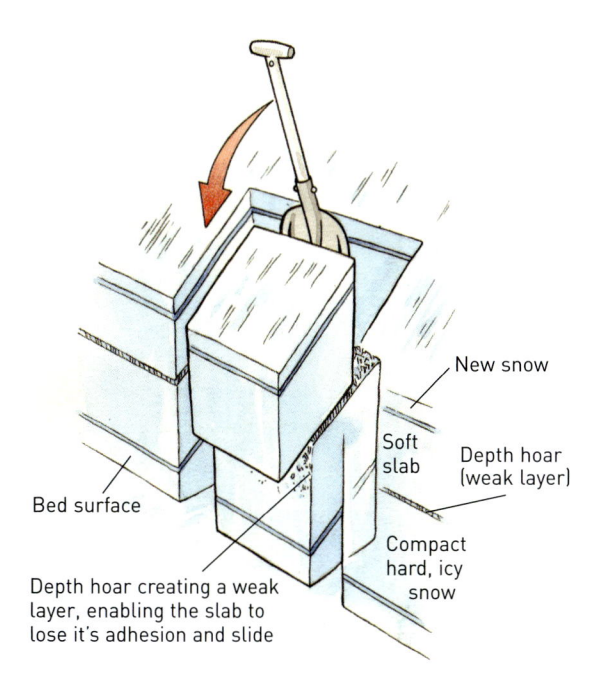

Fig. 20 The cohesiveness of layers can be judged using the shovel test.

THE LOADED COLUMN TEST

This must be done on a slope of 30 degrees or more and indicates how much weight must be applied before it fails.

- Isolate a column, but cut down to the bottom of the pit, and not just to the suspect layer.
- Flatten the top of the column and load it with blocks of snow the same size as the column until it fails or has enough snow to give you confidence it is not going to fail.

RUTSCHBLOCK TEST

This is the snow pit test of choice for those skiers who dig a lot of snow pits (Fig. 21). On a slope of at least 30 degrees, which is representative of the slope you are about to ski, isolate a block of snow about a ski-length across, and a ski-pole length up the slope. Do this by first cutting the face of the block using your shovel, then cut out the back and sides of the block using a ski tail (a snow saw can make the job quicker). Next, step on to the block with your skis and jump progressively harder until the block fails.

The large sample size makes the Rutschblock test more reliable, it duplicates what happens with a skier on the slope and it is easier to quantify and interpret. Rank the test on a scale of 1–7; the higher the number, the more stable the conditions. Ideally, you're looking for a score of 5 or more:

1. Fails while isolating the block
2. Fails while stepping onto the block
3. Fails with a light weighting of the skis
4. Fails with one light jump
5. Fails with one hard jump
6. Fails with several hard jumps
7. Doesn't fail

SNOWPACK TESTS

After doing the test, edge towards the slope you are going to ski, probing with your ski pole to check that the consistency of the snow is the same as the test area.

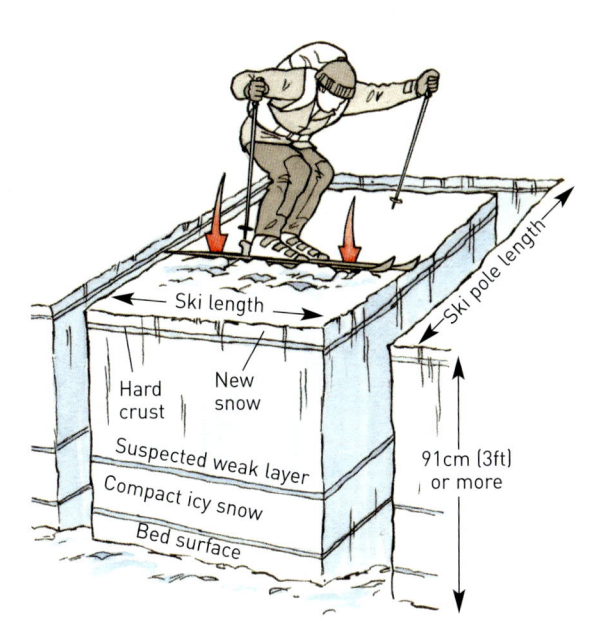

Fig. 21 The Rutschblock test

CROSSING A SUSPECT SLOPE

If you do have to cross a dangerous slope, ask yourself if it can be avoided.

- Lower someone on a rope to examine it.
- If you have to go ahead:
    - Remove ski straps
    - Zip up clothing and cover your mouth
    - Take your hands out of ski pole straps
    - If you are roped up, remove it, unless the risk of falling is greater than that of an avalanche.
- Team members should keep a minimum of 10m apart on traverses and 50m on descents or ascents to reduce the stress on the slope.
- If the risk is serious, cross one at a time, with everyone observing the person at risk – it is better to have four people searching for one, than one person searching for four!
- Maintain contact with each other, especially in poor visibility.
- Use the same track, and do not overtake other groups.
- Do not stop until you are at a safe haven such as a ridge, behind a very large rock buttress, within the shelter of large trees, or simply on a flat slope away from potential avalanche danger.
- Ensure that you watch the last person in the group across the slope.

CROSSING A SUSPECT SLOPE

WEAK SPOTS

Snow slopes are not uniform and the depth of snow varies. There may be buried rocks or vegetation where the temperature gradient and snow depth is different to your test area, which can trigger the slope to avalanche (see *Rucksack Guide: Winter Mountaineering*, A&C Black, 2009). The further down the weak layer is situated, the less likely you are to trigger an avalanche. They are rarely triggered when the weak layer is greater than 1.5m deep and you keep away from rocks or vegetation protruding from the snow.

Fig. 22 *Cross suspect slopes one at a time (skier Liz Richardson).*

IF YOU ARE CAUGHT IN AN AVALANCHE

Start fighting for your life! If you are not close to the surface and you have not created an air space, your chances of survival are slim.

- Run to the side of the avalanche, or jump upslope above the fracture.
- Do not release your bindings immediately – ski out of the avalanche to the closest edge. Should you fail, try to remove skis and poles, as they will drag you down (this is easier said than done!).
- If the slab is hard try to remain on top of a block.
- Recent evidence suggests that wearing a rucksack increases your surface area and keeps you higher in the avalanche.
- Shout!
- Try to remain on the surface using swimming movements, or try to roll like a log, off the debris.
- As the avalanche slows, make a desperate effort to get to the surface, or at least get a hand or ski pole through.
- Try to maintain an air pocket in front of your mouth and nose, clearing snow away from your mouth.
- Take and hold a deep breath at the last moment to maintain space for chest expansion.
- Try to avoid panicking to conserve your energy. Your companions will be searching for you.

SEARCHING FOR A BURIED VICTIM

Around 95 per cent of survivors are rescued by their companions. The several minutes it will take to call for help is better-spent searching.

DURING THE AVALANCHE
Watch and note where the victim was last seen, using landmarks such as rocks and trees. This can eliminate a whole section of the slope from your search.

AFTER THE AVALANCHE
- Start searching immediately.
- Be disciplined: someone must take charge and panic helps nobody.
- How many are missing? Spot clothing, equipment, and body parts protruding from the snow (remember that equipment may not necessarily indicate the victim's position).
- Appoint searchers to find the victims and rescuers to dig out and attend to victims. Switch the searcher's transceivers to 'search' and switch all other transceivers off.
- While transceivers are switched off, there is a high risk that if a subsequent avalanche buries someone they will not be found. Place guards high up the slope to give adequate warning of further avalanches and to determine a safe way out of the avalanche area.
- Those not involved in the search must stay high in a safe region and keep their skis on.

AVALANCHE SEARCH PHASES

SAFE ROUTE FINDING

The techniques used are broadly the same for any transceiver. There are three phases to every search:

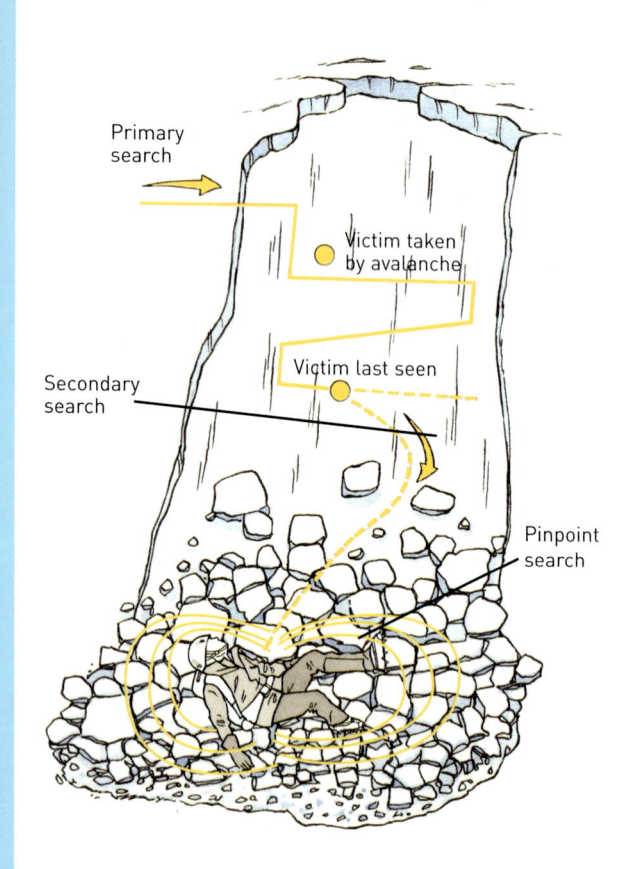

- Primary search
- Victim taken by avalanche
- Victim last seen
- Secondary search
- Pinpoint search

***Fig. 23** Primary, secondary and pinpoint search (thank you to the Alpine Ski Club for help with the diagrams. See www.alpineskiclub.org.uk for more information).*

AVALANCHE SEARCH PHASES

PRIMARY SEARCH
The aim is just to find the signal from the victim's transceivers. If you switch your transceiver to 'search' and you have a signal, you have completed the primary search.

- Switch the rescuers' transceivers to receive/search mode.
- Do a sweep search, from the level of the party, side-to-side down the track of the avalanche, traverses and kick-turns, with the line of each traverse ending no more than 20m from the previous line, until the transceiver starts to beep. Turn no more than 10m from the edge of the avalanche track.
- During the primary search, slowly rotate your beacon in all orientations (i.e. twist your wrist 360 degrees) to increase the likelihood that your antennae will align with the victim's. This rotation is especially important if you have a single antenna transceiver.
- If the avalanche is large, it may be more appropriate for two or more searchers to make parallel searches.
- When a signal is received, home in on the nearest (strongest) signal.
- If there is more than one victim, continue the primary search, even after the first contact, in order to discover victims who may be near the other side of the avalanche and to avoid having to search uphill later.

SECONDARY SEARCH
After you have found a signal, the aim is to get within 3m of the victim. The secondary search technique varies depending on whether you have a single or multiple-antenna transceiver. Here, I only consider the multiple-antenna approach.

AVALANCHE SEARCH PHASES

- When you have a signal, you may be up to 35m from the nearest victim.
- If the distance numbers increase (or the audible signal decreases), turn around and follow the direction indicator (or audible signal) in the opposite direction.
- As you move, slowly reorientate the transceiver, so that the arrow is pointing in line with the transceiver. The transceiver indicator lights point along the curved magnetic field lines. The range display shows how far you are along the field lines from the target transceiver.
- For more than one victim, the transceiver finds signals for all of them and the lights indicate their directions more or less alternately, depending on how fast each target transceiver sends its 'beep'.
- Head for the closest victim first. As you close in on a victim, modern transceivers lock to the strongest signal so only one victim is indicated.
- Transceivers beep at roughly one-second intervals and the receiving transceiver can only display one at a time, so take your time to identify the victim positions accurately. If you are descending, this should be the highest victim on the slope.
- If weaker, more distant signals are lost, mark the point (split point) with a ski pole, so that you can return there later to resume the search.
- The line followed will curve, since the transceiver follows the field lines of the victim's transceiver.
- As you get closer, the beeps become more frequent, and the tone changes until a high-pitched, rapid beeping indicates that you are very close.
- Ensure the range indicated is always getting smaller and is not increasing again.

AVALANCHE SEARCH PHASES

Fig. 24 Curved magnetic lines are created by the victim's transceiver.

PINPOINT SEARCH

Once you are within 3m of the victim, the aim is to get as close to the victim as possible. If there is more than one rescuer, only one should do the pinpoint search. The other should get ready to probe and dig. If there is more than one victim, additional rescuers should start a multiple burial search.

- At about 3m from the victim, tip the transceiver towards the ground at about 45 degrees, but do not swing your arms around.
- As you come close or cross the victim, stop and search carefully with the device close to the snow surface. The victim might be buried deep below your feet. Tipping the transceiver gives a better indication of the victim's position in the snow and the display will indicate how deeply they are buried.
- If you overshoot, the range will start to increase and the direction indication might become erratic (and then you will have to backtrack).
- When it is time to dig, do not put the transceiver down on the snow; instead, loop the strap around your neck and stuff the unit down your sleeve, or the front of your trousers.

MULTIPLE BURIAL SEARCH

If there are more victims buried and you can't turn off the transmitter of the victim just found, use the three circle search method to locate nearby victims, or return to the 'split point' (p. 54) to resume the search for more distant victims.

The three circle method searches in three concentric circles around the victim who was just found, and it works for all types of transceiver:

- Step away 3m (the length of an avalanche probe) from the victim already found.
- Search in a circle of radius 3m around the victim already found, slowly scanning the transceiver across the slope as you search, until you find the next victim.
- If no victim is found on this search increase the circle radius to 6m and repeat the search.
- Should no victim be found again, increase the circle radius to 9m and repeat the search. The diameter of this circle (18m) approximates to the 20m search track interval used on the initial search.
- Should you still fail to find the buried victim resume a new primary, secondary and pinpoint search.

AVALANCHE SEARCH PHASES

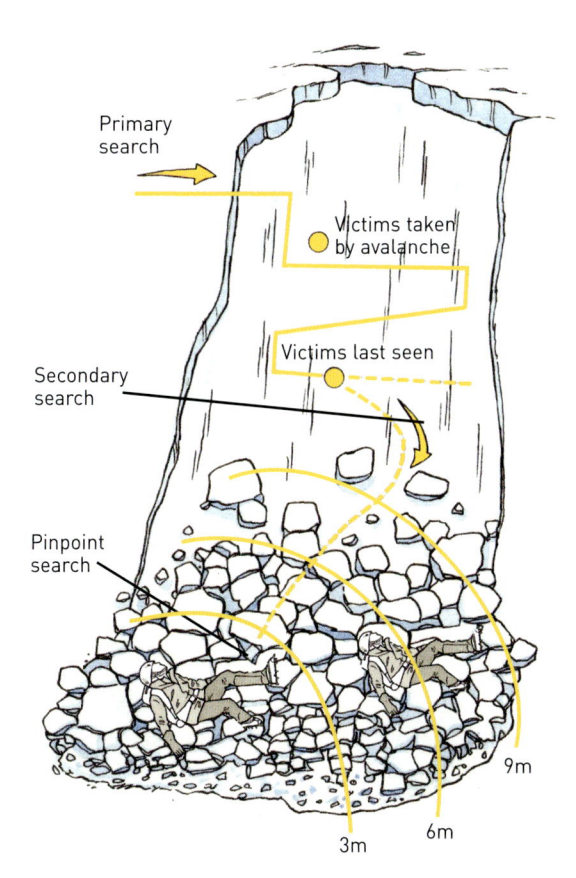

Fig. 25 The three circle method

DIGGING AND PROBING

Using an avalanche probe limits the amount of snow that has to be excavated. Since the pinpoint search is done along the snow surface, insert your probe perpendicular to the surface, and not straight down. Probe in a grid – not randomly – at 30cm intervals. After striking the victim, leave a probe in place and start shovelling downhill of the probe. Dig out victims that are close to the surface first: the shallow buried victim might be able to help dig out the deep burial.

- Keep your transceiver attached to your body when digging – don't lay it on the snow. Use it to frequently confirm the position of the victim.
- Do not trample on the victim's air space.
- Start digging 1.5 times the burial depth on the downhill side and towards the probe. The slot you are digging should be 2m wide to enable the victim to be rolled into the recovery position, or on to their back for artificial respiration.

Fig. 26 *Searching for an avalanche victim must be done quickly and efficiently.*

AVALANCHE SEARCH PHASES

- Throw snow to the side and when you are waist-deep, throw it downhill.
- If there are two diggers, dig side-by-side.
- Dig in relays and rotate diggers every few minutes.
- Slice the snow into blocks; do not try to lever it out as the handle of your shovel may break.
- If the burial is deep, dig in tiers. Diggers on each tier should remove snow dug from lower tiers.
- Clear space around the victim's face and chest as soon as you can and clear snow from the mouth and airway.
- Resuscitate the victim if necessary.
- Turn off the victim's transceiver.
- Insulate the victim from the snow, but leave them in the hole until proper insulation and evacuation can take place.
- Keep the victim warm.

WHEN YOU HAVE NO SIGNAL
Probe in likely burial spots – the fall line below where the victim was last seen; around the victim's equipment on the surface; and above and below rocks and trees, depressions, curves and the toe of the debris pile. Because victims rarely survive more than 2m down, probe multiple shallow areas rather than probing one or two areas deeply.

AFTER THE RESCUE

When all victims are found, return everyone to a place of safety, account for all members of the group, switch transceivers back to transmit and check them before setting off. Decide upon a safe evacuation route, which may even be down the avalanche. If professional help is required:

- Use a mobile phone in preference to sending someone for help. Alpine huts and ski lifts have telephones and emergency equipment.
- Make sure the rest of the group are safe and stay put until required.
- Identify your position clearly to the professionals.
- Clearly identify injuries and the help required.

Preparing for rescue by helicopter

Helicopters cannot land on heavily angled slopes. A flat area of about 5m square is ideal, with enough clearance for the helicopter's blades and tail in a 180-degree arc (hollows are not a good idea!) A helicopter tilts forward on take-off, so high ground that slopes away under the tail is best.

- If the helicopter is light enough to descend vertically or horizontally, only enough room to hover is required. If it is heavy a clear flight path is necessary.
- Mark your location with bright objects (the flash gun on your camera can be used to great effect).
- If the ground is steep, the helicopter will have to hover with the skids touching the ground.
- If it is very steep there is a danger of the rotors hitting the slope. It is likely it will drop off a rescuer and then depart until told to return. Hovering is risky when close to the ground.

AVALANCHE SEARCH PHASES

- Helicopters perform better if they can take off and land into the wind. Therefore, indicate the wind direction using streamers or stand with your back to the wind, arms pointing in the direction the wind is blowing.
- Stay clear of the landing zone.
- If visibility is poor, a reference, such as a person or pack, on the pilot's side of the helicopter can be useful. Disturb the snow to allow the pilot to see it.
- Do not try to touch the helicopter or cable before it has made contact with the ground. Static charges build up in a helicopter when it is flying and this is discharged when the helicopter or a cable touches the ground (they can jump a metre).
- The noise and dust from a helicopter is great – protect your eyes and ears.
- Stay away from the helicopter and only approach from the front when signalled to do so in single file.
- Drag, rather than carry, equipment such as skis.

Fig. 27 Helicopters rescue stricken skiers quickly, but they cannot always fly because of the weather.

If you were to avoid the risk of being caught in an avalanche entirely, you would rarely venture into the mountains on skis. If you follow the advice about choosing a safe route, the mountains can, however, be visited at almost any time with relative safety. Start by skiing easier-angled slopes and work towards those that are steeper. Enter a slope from the top, not the sides (especially under a cornice), and ski the edge of slopes before running the centre.

BEFORE LEAVING

You have planned your route, checked the avalanche conditions and packed your rucksack and food. In addition, remember the following each day:

- Wear your transceiver under your outer layer where it cannot be damaged or torn off. If you remove clothing due to warm weather, move your transceiver under your remaining clothes.

- Test that all transceivers are transmitting; it isn't good enough that the light is blinking. One member should ski away with his transceiver in receive mode and on maximum volume (range). Each member should then ski slowly past (10m away). If the signal is weak, replace the batteries.

- Turn all mobile phones off.

- Check that everyone has a shovel and that there are probes in the group.

- Ensure that everyone in the group knows where they are going, because they might need to find their own way out.

- Wear a harness unless you are definitely on unglaciated terrain – you never know when it might be needed.

- For more information on alpine mountaineering, see *Rucksack Guide: Alpinism* (2009).

Approaching the Dix hut, Switzerland

SNOW TYPES

On a typical ski tour you will encounter several types of snow depending on the prevailing weather conditions and orientation of the slope to the Sun.

- **Corn snow** Formed by repeated thawing and nightly refreezing of the surface. This alters the snow-crystal shape, producing snow similar to wet granular snow, but larger. It is a delight to ski.

- **Crust** A hard surface on top of softer snow, created by freezing rain, direct sunlight or wind loading. This packs down the upper layers of the snowpack, but leaves lower layers generally unaffected. A horror to ski.

- **Firn/neve snow** Snow that has undergone freeze-thaw cycles and solidifies, creating good skiing conditions.

- **Granular snow** Small pellets that may be wet (can form a snowball), or drier loose granular snow. Wet granular conditions are often found in the springtime. Confused with corn snow, but can be a delight to ski.

- **Ice** True ice conditions are rare. Much of what is perceived to be ice is actually wet granular snow that has refrozen to form a very dense surface.

- **Powder** Light, fluffy snow found during and immediately after a snowstorm – the stuff of dreams.

Find the best snow by finding the right slope for the time of day (skier: Andy Perkins, IFMGA Guide, Chamonix, France).

ASPECT

Finding the best snow is a case of finding the right slope for the time of day and a question of aspect, angle and elevation.

The changes in the snowpack are related to how much sun the slope receives and the air temperature.

- North-facing slopes keep snow conditions longer.
- East-facing slopes catch the morning sun when the air is cold and changes are slower.
- West-facing slopes catch the sun in the warm afternoon.
- East- and south-facing slopes tend to soften first, then west-facing slopes generally soften by midday; the powder will then begin to settle and change very quickly.
- As the weather warms up, the surface of the snow on south-, then west- and east-facing slopes will melt and refreeze during the night, forming a crust.
- South-facing slopes then melt during the day, but on other slopes you may need to wait for the crust to become thick enough to ski without breaking through or to melt away. Be careful not to assume southerly aspects are safer, because these crusts can grow weak layers.
- During the spring when the sun is stronger all slopes, except sheltered north-facing couloirs, thaw around mid-morning, giving excellent skiing.
- If conditions are cloudy, there may be no overnight refreeze and slopes will be skiable, but there is a greater risk of wet snow avalanches. Rock and serac fall is also a danger and snow bridges over crevasses will be weaker.
- When the wind is strong, the snow is stripped from windward slopes leaving a hard, icy surface, often with small ridges that are difficult to ski. When the wind-blown snow lands on lee slopes, soft or hard slabs may form.

ALTITUDE

- It is colder and windier the higher you go.
- Slopes without wind will hold powder longer.
- Lower altitudes are generally warmer so the melt-freeze cycle can make them safer earlier.

Fig. 28 Ski touring in Switzerland. Just after snowfall, powder is found on all slopes.

EXPERT TIP

Alun Richardson IFMGA Guide
www.freedomphotographs.co.uk

'Sit with your map and draw lines on those slopes with the potential for good snow to save time later.'

ANGLE

- Generally steeper slopes that face the Sun melt and freeze quicker than lower-angled slopes, so the snow will change faster.
- In deep snow it can be a fine line between having a slope steep enough to turn on, yet shallow enough to be safe.
- Steep slopes can make 20cm of fresh snow feel knee deep.
- Lower-angled slopes are better in crusty conditions, because you then stay on the top when turning.

ESTIMATING SLOPE ANGLE (Fig. 29)

Use two identical ski sticks to measure the angle of the slope (mark halfway on your ski pole to make life easy):

- Place the first pole vertically in the snow.
- Hold the second pole at a right angle (90 degrees) to the first so that it is horizontal.
- Adjust the height of the second pole until it touches the slope.
- Using the major angles and these easy-to-estimate ratios, estimate the angle of the slope:

    1:½ = 27 degrees
    1:¾ = 37 degrees
    1:1 = 45 degrees

- For slopes greater than 45 degrees do the opposite and move the vertical pole along the horizontal one.

Fig. 29 *Using ski sticks to measure the angle of the slope – this slope is approximately 30 degrees (skier Andy Perkins, IFMGA Guide).*

ASSESSING GRADIENTS FROM A DISTANCE

Observe the climbing tracks of other skiers; most tend to start kick-turning when slopes reach 30 degrees. Some people are uncomfortable skiing down a slope steeper than 30 degrees and may do kick-turns in descent.

You can also estimate minimum slope angle from avalanches, as loose snow avalanches often start spontaneously on slopes greater than 35 degrees.

SKIING TECHNIQUE

There isn't the space to examine technique in detail, but the best advice is that no matter what the snow is like, stay centred over your ski at all times. By weighting the centre of the ski, you enable it to perform as it was designed. Leaning forwards or backwards puts the weight on to your toes or your heel and, therefore, a different part of the ski.

To feel this, try stretching and bending movements with a rucksack on without moving your centre of balance from the centre of your ski. Focus on your knees and ankles.

To turn, keep your shoulders pointing down the slope, and tilt your ski to edge it by swinging your hip smoothly towards the centre of the turn. The amount will depend on the turn and your speed. Try to pivot your foot from the centre of the ski.

EXPERT TIP

Eric Pirie
BMG/IFMGA Mountain Guide
E_pirie@talk21.com

'Always keep your skis flat on the snow when you are skinning – more surface area contact means more grip. Should you feel them starting to slip back, stand up tall and feel you are pushing down through your heels.'

***Fig. 30** Lorenz Frutiger showing good ski technique*

When the slope is too steep to skin up or there is not enough snow, you will have to carry your skis. Here are several techniques.

LOOSELY TIED
- Load your skis individually on each side, as low as possible and with the tips free.
- This is useful when travelling through trees, as the skis are unlikely to catch on overhead branches.

CARRYING SKIS

Fig. 31 The high A-frame carry (skier Owen Cox)

THE HIGH AND LOW A-FRAME

- Loading the skis high up is best for most situations, especially abseiling, but beware that it does raise your centre of gravity.
- Loading the skis lower down is better in high winds or when scrambling, because it lowers your centre of gravity. However, the skis can catch the backs of your legs.

CARRYING SKIS

THE DIAGONAL BACK SLING
- Bind your skis together first.
- This is useful when you are removing the skis regularly.

Fig. 32 *The diagonal back-sling carry (skier Andy Perkins, IFMGA Guide)*

Skinning towards the Barre des Ecrins Dauphine, Alps, France

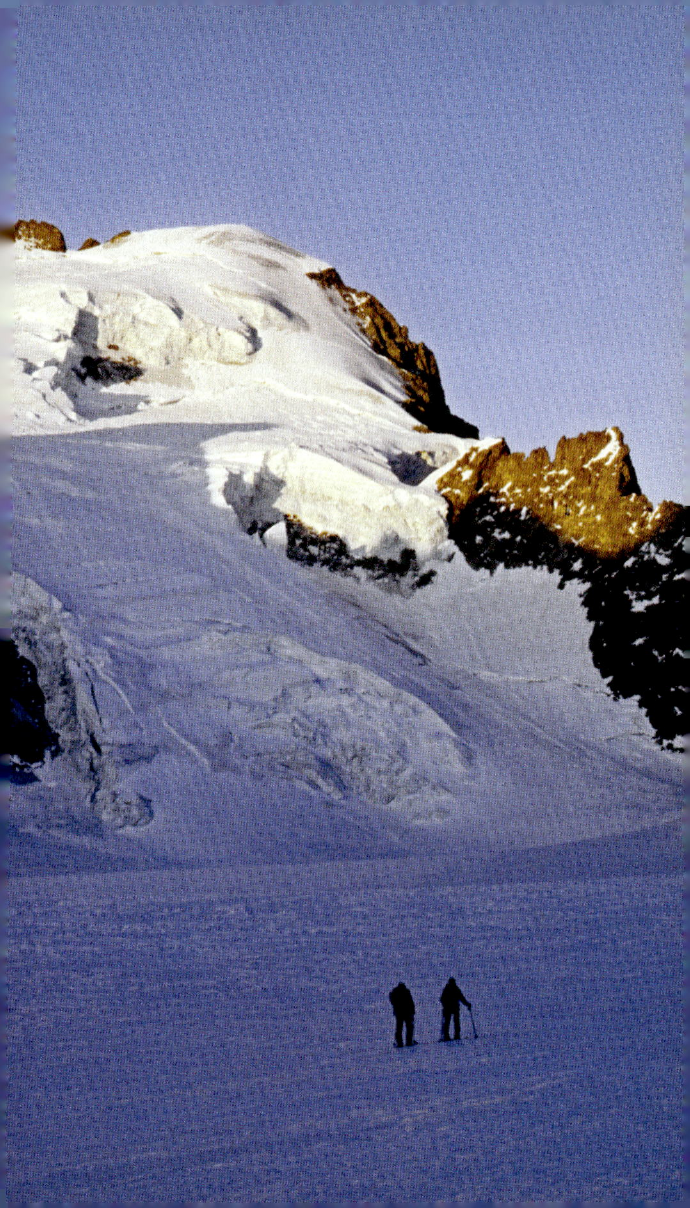

CARE AND USAGE

Skins are the equivalent of a Vibram sole on a walking boot. They should not come off the ski, unless the ski is wet or your skinning technique is poor. Most importantly, maintain the stickiness of the glue by keeping the skins as clean, warm and dry as possible. After use, fold each end of each skin into the middle so that it sticks to itself, or attach them on to the clear plastic sheets that they are supplied with.

Do not remove skins with your skis still on. It may be useful if you are ski racing, but it increases the chance of the skin becoming wet. It is also easier to stick the skins to a plastic cover when the skin is still half attached to the ski. Trying to put skins on while wearing skis is also pointless, because it is difficult to smooth the skin down and dry the ski.

CARE AT A HUT OR TENT
- Hang skins up folded so that the glue cannot attract any dust.
- If you are camping, take skins into your sleeping bag at night.
- Do not leave skins drying on your skis, especially in the Sun or a warm room, because the glue can transfer to the ski base, which makes skiing downhill difficult.

PREPARATION
- Dry the ski base and ensure that the skins are stuck on by firmly smoothing them down the length of each ski.
- Pay attention to the front and back of the ski base, which is where most problems occur.
- Start moving as soon as possible; the pressure will help the skins to stick.

LOOKING AFTER SKINS WHEN SKIING
- Keep your skins warm when skiing downhill by placing them under your clothes.
- If it is warm, carry them in the top pocket of your rucksack.

WHEN A SKIN COMES OFF
- Stick the skin back on with duct tape as soon as possible.
- Once a skin has totally unpeeled you have a real problem, because the glue must be free of snow and water to stick again.
- If the skin has completely detached, first rub the glued side across your thigh to get as much moisture off as possible; or plant a ski firmly in the snow, wrap the skin around the ski with the glue towards the base, then drag the skin back and forth over an edge.
- If possible, hang it up with the glue facing the Sun.
- In extreme circumstances you can use a lighter to warm the glue.
- Dry the ski, and if all else fails try double-sided sticky tape or a can of Coll Tex quick glue spray.

BALLING UP

On warm days, particularly after fresh snowfall, skins can collect snow. Pre-treating them with Coll Tex skin wax, standard ski wax or at a push candle wax, helps to reduce the problem and enhances their glide properties. At the first sign of balling:

- Stamp your feet with each stride.
- If it all gets too much, de-ball them by rubbing a ski pole up and down the bases.
- If you have a block of wax, use it now to prevent it happening again a short while later.
- Various glide sprays that do the same thing are available, but the skin must be dry, and they do not last as long or work as well.
- After going through water, stop and use the edge of another ski to scrape excess water off before it turns to ice.

Fig. 33 Balling up is a problem after fresh snowfall followed by a hot day.

MAINTENANCE

LONGER-TERM MAINTENANCE
- Store skins in airtight bags to prevent the glue drying out between trips.
- To check the glue, fold your skins together, and then try to pull them apart. If it is easy to do, especially around the tail, re-glue the skins.
- New glue can be applied on top of the old glue several times but, if you have time, remove and put new glue on.
- Remove glue using a solvent and scraper, or a soldering iron modified with a flat blade scraper and thermostat controller.
- Alternatively, place newspaper over the glued surface and warm it with an iron – the glue transfers to the paper. Repeat with clean sheets until it has all come off.
- Glue should be applied thinly and left to dry overnight in a warm room.
- It is also possible to buy iron-on glue.

EXPERT TIP

Bruce Goodlad
BMG/IFMGA Guide

'On multi-day ski tours carry at least one spare skin. A standard skin will not fit modern skis, therefore split one up the middle, 5cm in from the tip and all the way to the tail. When it is attached, you can follow the edge of the ski.'

SKINNING TECHNIQUE

A ski, binding and boot can weigh 5kg, so good skinning technique will keep your legs fresh for the downhill run.

- Glide the ski forward smoothly and rhythmically, without lifting, by sliding one ski forward in a long, but not too long, stride.
- Rolling your hips slightly can help to put pressure alternatively on each ski.
- The heel on your rear boot should rise until the sole is almost vertical, but you can still maintain pressure.
- Then push the rear ski forward by applying slight pressure on the centre, so that the skin maintains contact with the snow as it glides forward.
- Keep the tip of your ski a metre or two from the tail's of the person in front of you.
- As the slope steepens, more pressure must be applied to keep the skins in contact with the snow.
- Look ahead, not at your ski tips, and keep your chin up and your shoulders back, which will ensure your weight stays at the rear allowing you to maintain more pressure on the centre of your ski.
- You can lessen the strain on your calf muscles by taking shorter strides, pushing with the sticks behind you and using the heel lifts to maintain a more level ski. Heel lifts also reduce blistering and chafing.
- When the slope angle becomes greater than 30 degrees you should zigzag, following the line of least resistance (see selecting a line and kick turning p.90).

SKINNING TECHNIQUE

Fig. 34 *When skinning on a hard snow surface, avoid edging your skis, because this will soon lead to strenuous side-stepping. Instead, roll your ankles and knees slightly down the hill (skier Bruce Goodlad, IFMGA Guide).*

SKINNING TECHNIQUE

ON HARD SNOW
On hard snow, edging your skis will soon lead to strenuous side-stepping. Instead, roll your ankles and knees slightly down the hill, so that the skin is in contact with the snow (Fig. 34) – rather like flat footing when wearing crampons. Using heel lifts makes this difficult, so keep them low in these conditions. If the line of least resistance is too steep and the snow too hard to do this, the answer lies with harscheisen.

Fig. 35 Using heel lifts can reduce calf strain on steeper slopes.

USING HARSCHEISEN

On moderate slopes of hard snow, harscheisen make skinning easier by reducing the need to roll the ankle. However, they are not worth wearing on easy-angled slopes, as they reduce glide and restrict the stride. They are also not designed for use on water ice or rock, which can bend the soft metal teeth. If the consequences of a slip are serious, remove your skis and use crampons.

If you use Fritschi Diamir bindings, the harscheisen come off the snow when you raise your heel, so keep your heel lifts lower to improve crampon contact. Do not be tempted to ski downhill with your ski crampons folded upwards, or still in place – they will seriously affect your skiing.

Fig. 36 *Harscheisen are better for use on moderate slopes of hard snow.*

> **DESCENDING ON SKINS**
>
> The additional drag created by the skins can increase control when descending very steep slopes, but they do reduce the manoeuvrability of the ski, which creates its own problems.

USING POLES

Efficient use of your ski poles save energy.

- Keep your hands out of the leashes to save time on turns and avoid snagging in trees.
- On uphill traverses, the uphill hand should hold the pole lower down and the downhill hand should push on the top of the pole.
- Keep your arms close to your sides.
- When you reach forwards, plant your pole with straight arms – your poles will naturally tilt a bit. This will propel you forwards, directing your energies to moving uphill, and not side to side.
- The ski pole basket should plant near the middle of your back foot.

SKINNING TECHNIQUE

SKINS AND SKINNING

Fig. 37 Skinning towards the top of Lesley's Peak, Greenland

TRACK SETTING WHEN SKINNING

An effective track minimises kick turns, reduces the ups and downs, avoids areas where grip may be poor, such as ice or soft snow, and minimises exposure to hazards.

- In deep snow, the track will feel very steep to the lead skier, but the followers will find the angle quite comfortable as the snow is flattened, so change the lead skier frequently.
- It is best to choose a line where you can make a smooth walking turn that does not require a kick turn.
- Look for softer snow, flat areas near trees, bumps, or other terrain irregularities that will allow a smooth, easy turn, rather than a sharp, difficult one.

Charlie Sommerfield and Gareth Richardson skinning in the Alps

SKINNING TECHNIQUE

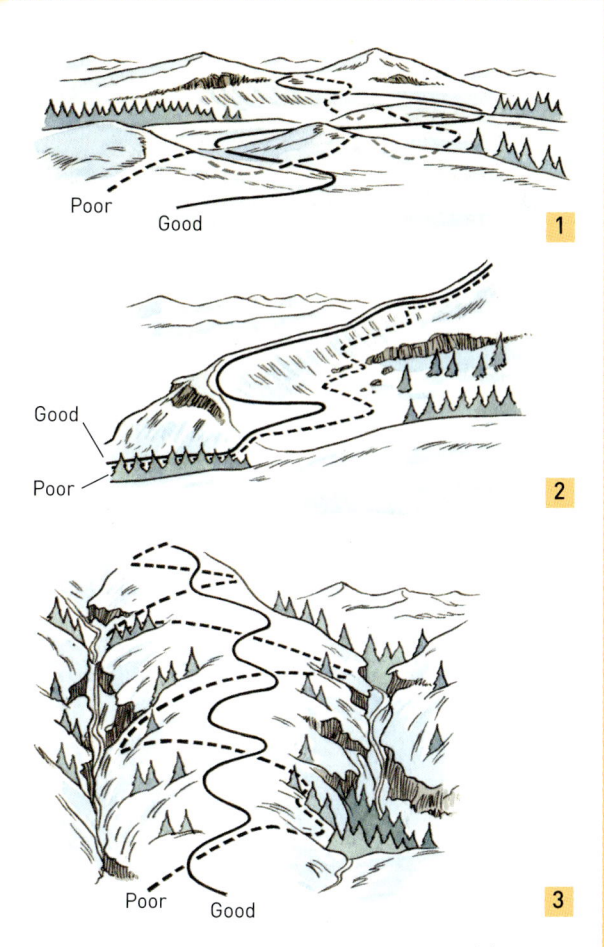

Fig. 38 *Good and poor track setting on hilly terrain (1), a ridge crest (2) and a broad ridge (3).*

Fig. 39 *Experienced skinners seek a balance between efficiency and safety and know how to set a track that takes the path of least resistance.*

SKINNING TECHNIQUE

SKINS AND SKINNING

TURNING ON STEEP SLOPES

You will eventually ascend slopes so steep that you cannot easily walk around the turn. At this point, you will have to lift one ski, place it in the new direction, weight it and lift the other one around.

THE DOWNHILL KICK TURN

This is a defensive technique that is useful when the snow conditions are too horrible to ski. It can also be used when ascending, but you lose height and, if you are using a rope it is difficult. This technique is done more easily with the bindings in 'downhill mode'.

1 Face downhill with your skis perpendicular to the slope.
2 Place your poles behind you on the uphill slope to provide support.
3 With your weight on the ski poles, lift the downhill ski, and rotate it to face in the new direction.
4 Move the ski in close to the uphill ski and stamp to set it in the snow.
5 Move the uphill ski into the new direction.
6 Point the tip downhill to help the tail clear the uphill snow.

In hard or crusty snow the downhill kick-turn can be modified by removing the ski on the downhill foot, making a kick-turn with one ski, and then replacing the ski on the uphill side after the turn is finished. If all else fails, remove both skis.

TURNING ON STEEP SLOPES

SKINS AND SKINNING

Fig. 40 The downhill kick-turn (skier Andy Perkins, IFMGA Guide)

TURNING ON STEEP SLOPES

STEP AROUND TURN (CLOCK TURN)
This is the next stage if the slope is too steep to walk around in a gentle curve.

1 As you approach the turn, stamp the lower ski to make a good platform.
2 Lift the uphill ski and place it in the new direction.
3 Weight it, and then bring the lower ski into the same direction.

Do this turn in a series of smaller changes, like the moving hands of a watch, without a break in your rhythm.

Fig. 41 The clock turn (skier B. Goodlad, IFMGA Guide)

Gareth Richardson

THE UPHILL KICK TURN (Fig. 42)

This is the most common method for changing direction uphill.

1. At the corner, stamp out a flat platform, perpendicular to the fall-line, and position the poles as shown in photo 1 opposite.
2. Move the uphill ski forward, lift the tip and turn it to the new direction.
3. Move the feet close together. Be sure the uphill ski is nearly level.
4. Reposition the outside pole for better stability, leaving enough room for the next ski to come around.
5. Transfer weight to the uphill ski.
6. Once you have the uphill ski in position and can balance on it, pick up the downhill ski and, in one continuous motion, 'clack' your heel against the ski to bring the tip up and push the tail down, while pivoting the ski into the new direction. You need to do the 'clack' with your foot behind you and your ski still pointing in the original direction. *Note:* Nordic skiers should set their bindings more for a touring mode (easy heel lift) and less for a downhill mode (harder heel lift).
7. Slide the ski into the track and off you go.

TURNING ON STEEP SLOPES 95

SKINS AND SKINNING

Fig. 42 Uphill kick-turn for changing direction when travelling uphill (skier B. Goodlad, IFMGA Guide)

TURNING ON STEEP SLOPES

THE ALTERNATIVE UPHILL KICK-TURN (Fig. 43)
When the track is in deep snow and/or the slope is steep or there is an obstacle above you at the turn, it can be difficult to get the first ski around to face the new direction.

1 At the corner, stamp out a flat platform perpendicular to the fall-line, and place both poles on the uphill slope.
2 Lift the uphill ski and drop it downhill behind you.
3 Pivot the tail downhill as the ski tip clears the downhill ski boot.
4 Turn it 180 degrees into the new direction, and place it below what was originally the downhill ski.
5 Transfer your weight to the new downhill ski and stamp it to be sure it won't move. The poles are moved slightly for better balance as the right foot (uphill ski) is un-weighted.
6 Pick up your uphill ski, clear the tail past your other boot, then 'clack' and follow through as per the regular kick-turn.

TURNING ON STEEP SLOPES

SKINS AND SKINNING

Fig. 43 The alternative kick-turn in deep tracks (skier B. Goodlad, IFMGA Guide)

TACTICS FOR SKIING SLOPES

The following assumes that all skiers are of equal ability.

- Ski with a partner, maintaining voice contact via leap-frogging or skiing in formation.
- It is easy to lose contact in trees (whistle frequently to maintain communication with your group).
- Stop at the bottom (the most experienced skier should stop first).
- Look for hazards such as sudden drops and crevasses.
- Stop well above a hazard and do not gather together on a glacier.
- In poor visibility, or when the terrain is serious, shorten the sections skied and follow the tracks of the more experienced skier to provide you with a reference point.
- Use yellow goggles or glasses in flat light.

Fig. 44 Always ski with a partner (Jay Taylor IFMGA Guide).

GENERAL TACTICS

SKIING SIGNALS

A clear set of signals will be important to direct the following skiers to the best snow or the safest line past a crevasse.

- Do not follow each other too closely and on suspect slopes you should descend one at a time.
- To indicate that it is okay to ski put your poles in a 'Y' shape above your head.

Fig. 45 Other common skiing signals: (1) move to the right until the poles are dropped before starting to ski; (2) do not ski the slope; and (3) ski, but stay right of me.

CONTROLLING SPEED IN STEEP TERRAIN

When the terrain becomes too steep or the snow to poor for you to ski in control, try the following:

- Drag your ski poles on a traverse
- Side slip
- Downhill kick-turn and traverse
- Hold both ski poles together and place them across your body into the slope
- Fan turn in soft snow – kick the tail of the skis into the snow and walk them round into a new direction.

FALLING ON SKIS

Falling on steep ground is the second most frequent cause of serious off-piste ski accidents. Sit rather than fall – the added weight of your pack can make it happen suddenly. If you do fall, and the consequence of a slide is serious, here are several methods to try.

The hip check fall

- Fall on to your hip sideways and uphill (keep your knees clear).
- Try to use your momentum to bounce immediately back up on to your skis so that you do not begin sliding.

The shoulder roll

- If you fall face-first, tuck into a somersault, roll and land back on your skis as quickly as possible.
- If you want to stop, land with your skis across the fall-line.
- If you want to recover, angle your skis down the fall-line.
- Practice on steep slopes that won't have serious consequences.

Claire Sommerfield perfecting the 'shoulder roll'.

Getting back up in deep snow
- If your skis have stayed on, place them flat across the fall-line, pack a platform and place your ski poles flat on the snow by your hip.
- Push down on the poles with the uphill hand and stand on to your skis. Someone can help by standing downhill of you and pulling on your downhill hand.
- If your skis have come off, create a platform, stick tails of your skis into the snow, keep them flat, clean snow from your boots and put on the downhill ski first.
- If you have lost a ski, try to determine its trajectory by looking for tracks. The ski is often higher than anticipated. Begin your search below the suspected point and use your ski poles to slice through the snow perpendicular to the line of travel.

The self-arrest
Self-arrest technique has two basic steps:

1 Get your skis below you quickly. Shoulder-roll or drag your hand or ski-pole grip out to one side, like a canoe paddle. With some effort, the skis will circle below you.
2 A natural response is to sit on your rear or lie flat on your stomach, but your clothing is likely to be slippery. Instead, arch your back and rear towards the sky; and push your ski-pole grips, fingers and ski edges into the snow. Try to get everything off the snow except for your hands and skis.

The value of using specialised ski pole self-arrest grips is questionable. They tend to rotate in your glove and end up facing towards your body. If you use them to arrest you must drive your shoulder into the grip head to help bury the pick, just as you must do with an ice axe.

SKIING IN CREVASSED TERRAIN

Ensure you understand glacial travel and rescue techniques before venturing into glaciated terrain and make sure you wear a harness (*see Rucksack Guide: Alpinism* (A&C Black, 2009).

During the winter there is often enough snow to allow you to ski over crevassed terrain with safety, and it is rare that teams rope up. Attach a sling and a krab to your harness and the shoulder of your rucksack to make it easier to attach a rescue rope should you end up down a crevasse. The safest method is to ski straight across crevasses.

- It is important that you give yourself time to react – keep everyone in sight and follow the tracks of the lead skier.
- Be wary of any new snow cover on glaciers.
- Keep your eyes open; don't just look down the fall-line, but spot crevasses out to the side of your descent line.
- If you crash in glaciated terrain and both skis have released, stay put and get someone else to retrieve them.
- If you must take a break in crevassed terrain, avoid walking around without your skis or stay roped-up 5m apart, and use your avalanche probe to check the area.

Fig. 46 Ski perpendicular to crevasses, and not along them.

SKIING ROPED UP

Skiing roped-up is a nightmare, even for experienced skiers. It slows you down and rope management on turns is difficult. However, it is a necessary evil when poor visibility is combined with skinning uphill on unfamiliar wet glaciers, especially during warm conditions; or when skiing downhill with shallow, low-density, or variable snow cover (particularly in early or late winter) and poor visibility.

ROPING UP WHEN SKINNING

On the uphill sections, all members of the rope team need to pause and manage the rope when any other member does a kick-turn. The technique for roping up is the same as for summer alpinism (see *Rucksack Guide: Alpinism* (A&C Black, 2009).

- Two 30m x 8mm nylon ropes (30m of Dyneema cord is sometimes carried) prevents one person carrying all of the rope.
- Three to a rope is better than two for holding a fall, but it makes managing the rope on turns more difficult.
- The second-strongest skier should be at the front and the strongest at the rear.
- Each member should carry at least one Wild Country Ropeman Mk II, Petzl Mini Traxion or similar device that will grip a thin rope more effectively than a prusik.
- Do not allow slack rope to develop and do not carry hand coils.

There are two methods for roping up (Fig. 47 and Fig. 48 opposite). See *Rucksack Guide: Alpinism* for further information.

SKIING ROPED UP 105

TACTICS FOR SKIING SLOPES

Fig. 47 Method one – roping up for glacial travel

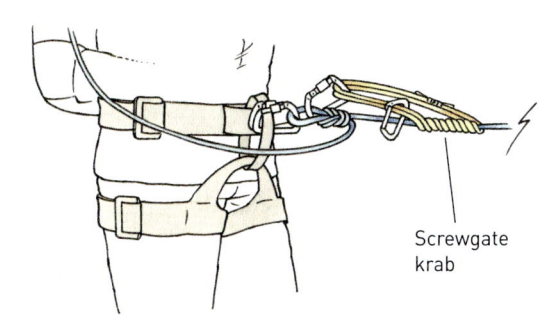

Screwgate krab

Fig. 48 Method two for tying into the end of a rope (the remainder of your rope is carried in your rucksack).

DESCENDING ROPED-UP
The only practical way to descend roped-up is in a very slow snowplough (Fig. 49).

- The second and third skiers shouldn't turn at the same place as the first: the second turns shortly after the first and the third shortly after the second, preferably in the same direction.
- The lead skier skis with a pole in each hand, while the second and third skiers carry both poles in one hand or stowed on the rucksack and manage the rope with the other (a sling attached to the rope via a prusik can help).
- The lead skier must take particular care not to speed up and catapult the other skiers off their feet.
- The strongest skier, or the one with the biggest thighs, should be at the back.
- When conditions allow, a preferable option to roping up the whole group is for the strongest skiers to rope up 25m apart and the rest of the team to follow in their tracks.

HOLDING A FALL
The aim of the skier holding the fall is to get their skis parallel to the crevasse. It is advisable to have your ice axe available by slotting it down your back in case you cannot remove your skis to make a belay.

SKIING ROPED UP 107

TACTICS FOR SKIING SLOPES

Fig. 49 Managing the rope when descending – note only the lead skier is holding both poles.

CREVASSE RESCUE

It is important that everyone has crevasse rescue kit easily available and wears a harness. The two people carrying the ropes must not ski together at the front.

- If the party is divided into two roped teams, the other team should quickly come forward and attach their rope to the victim's loaded rope via a Wild Country Ropeman or equivalent. This will allow the team holding the victim to create an anchor more easily.
- Once the anchor has been created, it is important for the rescuers to see the victim and, if possible, use another rope to retrieve the victim's skis and rucksack.

Fig. 50 Everyone should wear a harness and carry a crevasse rescue kit when skiing in crevassed terrain.

WHEN DOWN A CREVASSE

- Release your skis and rucksack and attach them to the rope. Hopefully rescuers are on their way and can haul them to make your escape easier.
- Without skis you may be able to crampon out, but it is important that you communicate first with the rescuers so that, should you fall, the belay system is not shock loaded.
- If all else fails, prusik out.

CREATING A RESCUE ANCHOR

Where the victim has fallen down the crevasse and cannot communicate, the rescuers must create an anchor strong enough to take the forces generated by a pulley system. Build a crevasse rescue anchor at the location of the skier nearest to the crevasse to reduce rope stretch. The closest skier can create the anchor, but in a team of three or more, this is best done by another skier moving forwards along the rope, using their prusik to keep the rope taut to assist the skier holding the victim should they start to slide forward.

SKI ANCHORS

The amount of soft snow in winter increases the difficulty of creating a secure anchor, and the extra snow increases friction in any crevasse rescue system. However, your skis can now be used to create an anchor.

There are two methods, depending on what the anchor is to be used for, the quality of the snow and whether you can remove your own skis. The first method is adequate for rescue when the snow is firm, or for an abseil or lower down a steep slope, but if the last person must also abseil, a snow mushroom may be better. If the anchor is to be used for crevasse rescue, method two is probably better.

CREATING A RESCUE ANCHOR

Method one (Figs 51 and 52)
This method is best-used in firm snow.

- The combination of two skis with their camber resisting the direction of pull makes for a very strong anchor that is quick to set up.

- Plunge the ski tails slightly back from the direction of pull, into the snow as far as you can, at least to the bindings (about 45cm) apart, perpendicular to the direction of pull with the metal edges facing downhill.

- To link the skis, attach the rope to the rear ski with a bowline, and then attach it horizontally to the front ski using a clove hitch.

- Leave some slack rope and attach the rope as low as possible on the front ski using a figure of eight knot. The same can also be created using slings (Fig. 52).

Fig. 51 Creating a ski anchor using the rope (note the orientation of the ski edge).

CREATING A RESCUE ANCHOR

Fig. 52 Creating a ski anchor using slings

Method two
This method is preferable when the snow is softer and the anchor is to be used for a hoist.

- Bury your skis horizontally, the same way you would bury an ice axe (see *Rucksack Guide: Winter Climbing*, A&C Black, 2009).
- Make sure the sharp metal edges of the skis are pointing towards the crevasse.
- You can also place a buried ice axe uphill of the skis.

CREATING A RESCUE ANCHOR

TRANSFERRING THE LOAD TO THE ANCHOR
(Fig. 53)

- Once an anchor has been created, the loaded rope is transferred to it by rolling towards the sling attached to the anchor.
- The spare screwgate krab hanging from the French prusik is then clipped into the anchor.
- Gently load the anchors by moving towards the crevasse.
- When you are confident the anchor is holding, remove the opengate krab from your harness and back-up the prusik by immediately clipping the rope to the anchor with a locking krab and a tied-off Italian hitch.

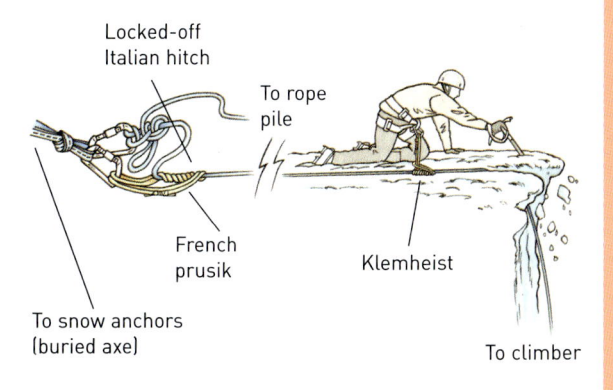

Fig. 53 Approaching the edge of the crevasse

AFTER THE LOAD IS TRANSFERRED

The rescuer can now move to the edge of the crevasse, protected by a prusik or ascender (Fig. 53), probing the snow to find the true edge of the crevasse. The edge of the crevasse will probably have to be prepared no matter what the next step (the exception may be if the victim's life is threatened, and speed is essential, or if the collapsing snow will injure them).

Remove overhanging snow to free the loaded rope, but take great care – a rope under tension is easily cut. Place a rucksack, ski pole or ice axe under the loaded rope at the edge and secure. Once the edge is prepared you have a number of options in order of preference:

- Lower the victim to somewhere they can climb out, or just to take the load from the rope.
- It may be possible for the victim to climb out of the crevasse while being belayed from above.
- Simply pull the victim out.
- Use a two-team pull.
- Prusik out.
- Hoist the victim...a last resort (p.116)!

The worst-case scenario is a seriously injured victim – the rescuer will need to abseil to them using the other end of the rope:

- Pad the lip of the crevasse under the abseil rope and take a first aid kit and warm clothing, or a sleeping bag, to treat and bundle the victim.
- The process of hauling out an unconscious victim can easily take over an hour (Fig. 54).
- After treatment, make an improvised chest harness and clip it to a prusik on their rope to keep them upright. To prevent the victim from suffocating by being dragged through the snow, turn them so that their back is against the wall of the crevasse. Retrieve any climbing gear the victim has with them, particularly prusiks, before ascending.

AFTER THE LOAD IS TRANSFERRED

CREVASSE RESCUE

Rescuer's rope is stopped from cutting into the edge of crevasse with padding under the rope

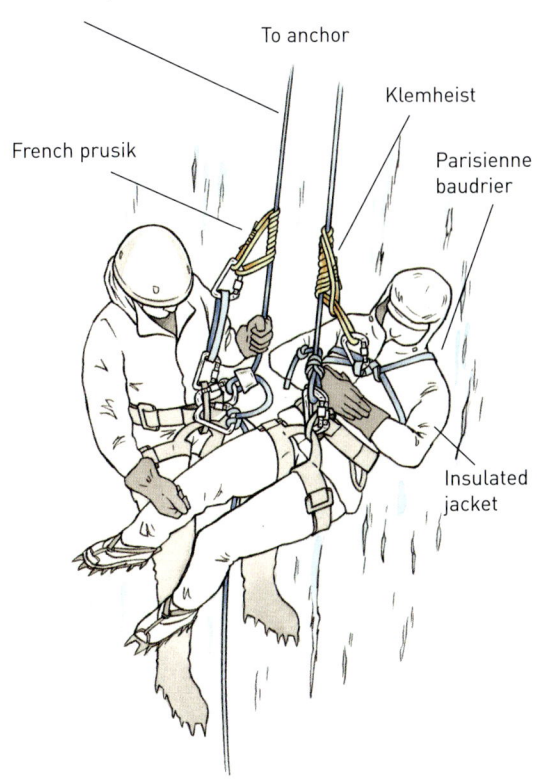

To anchor

Klemheist

French prusik

Parisienne baudrier

Insulated jacket

Fig. 54 *Descend to the victim and make them comfortable.*

SIMPLE PULL

If there are enough rescuers, simply pull the victim from the crevasse (rescuers should not walk backwards unless they are sure that they will not fall into another crevasse). The rope to the victim should be belayed or protected via a prusik or ascender attached to an anchor. If you feel resistance, do not pull anymore; the victim may be at the lip of the crevasse.

TWO-TEAM PULL

If another team is available, the first team arrests the fall and holds the victim while the second approaches the edge and sends a rescue rope to the victim. If this team can do this quickly it may not be necessary for the first team to build an anchor and transfer the load. If an anchor is not built, the first team belays the victim by moving backward in the self-arrest position as the second team hauls the victim usually using an assisted hoist.

PRUSIKING OUT

To prusik out:

- Remove your coils and undo them.
- Clip your rucksack and skis into the loop of rope below you or attach it via a knot.
- Attach a foot prusik to the rope and ascend.
- It may be prudent to drop the other end of the rope so the victim can prusik up the second line, rather than the line jammed into the snow.

Liz Richardson on Col du Chardonnet

HOISTING USING PULLEYS (Figs 55–57)

Now things get serious; any pulley system will put an enormous load on to anchors, and, because of friction at the lip of the crevasse, all hoisting is strenuous. The rope will usually cut deeply into the snow at the lip of the crevasse; whether this can be freed, how far the victim is into the crevasse, and whether the victim can help the rescuer will all dictate the method used.

All hoisting methods have pros and cons, and each follows the same principles as hoisting systems for rock climbing. **Note:** Remember to release the Italian hitch and place the rope back through the karabiner before hoisting.

- Whenever possible, use the spare rope to get the victim out, because the loaded rope (if the victim is wearing one) will have bitten into the snow on the edge of the crevasse.

- An assisted hoist with a Ropeman (Fig. 55) or, better, a Petzl Mini Traxion is probably the fastest option when the victim is able to pull.

- Use an unassisted hoist as a last resort (Figs 56 and 57).

HOISTING A VICTIM

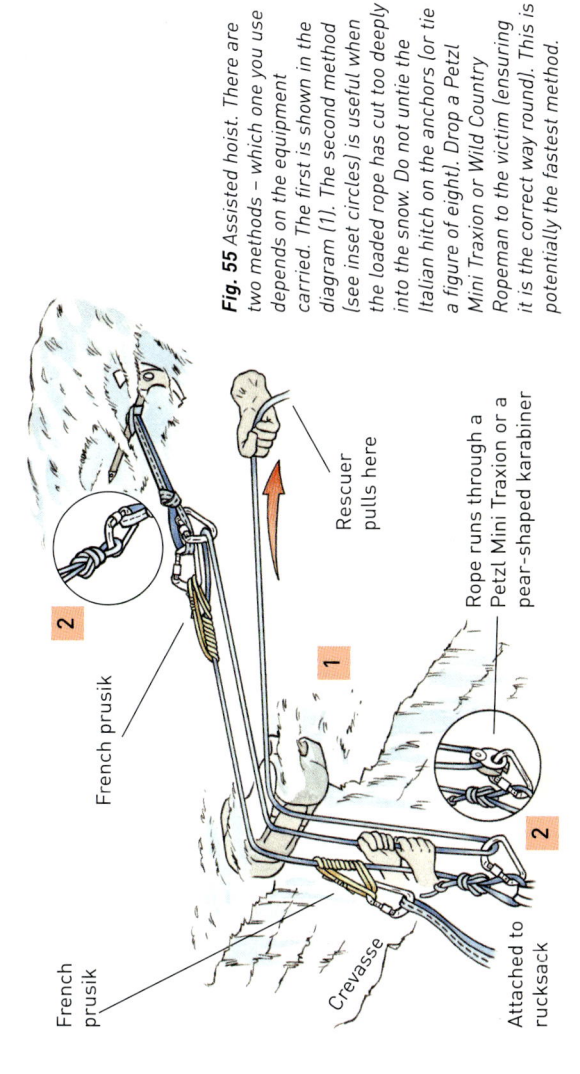

Fig. 55 Assisted hoist. There are two methods – which one you use depends on the equipment carried. The first is shown in the diagram (1). The second method (see inset circles) is useful when the loaded rope has cut too deeply into the snow. Do not untie the Italian hitch on the anchors (or tie a figure of eight). Drop a Petzl Mini Traxion or Wild Country Ropeman to the victim (ensuring it is the correct way round). This is potentially the fastest method.

Rescuer pulls here

Rope runs through a Petzl Mini Traxion or a pear-shaped karabiner

French prusik

French prusik

Attached to rucksack

Crevasse

120 HOISTING A VICTIM

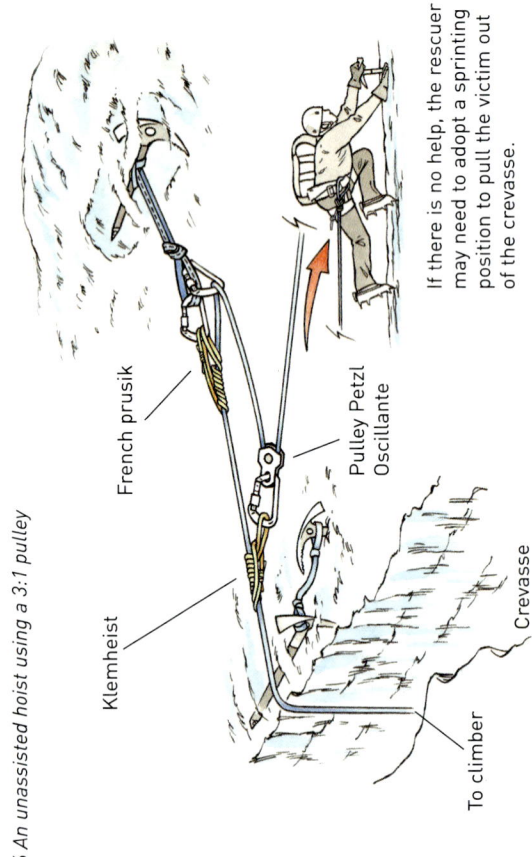

CREVASSE RESCUE

Fig. 56 *An unassisted hoist using a 3:1 pulley*

- Klemheist
- French prusik
- Pulley Petzl Oscillante
- To climber
- Crevasse

If there is no help, the rescuer may need to adopt a sprinting position to pull the victim out of the crevasse.

HOISTING A VICTIM

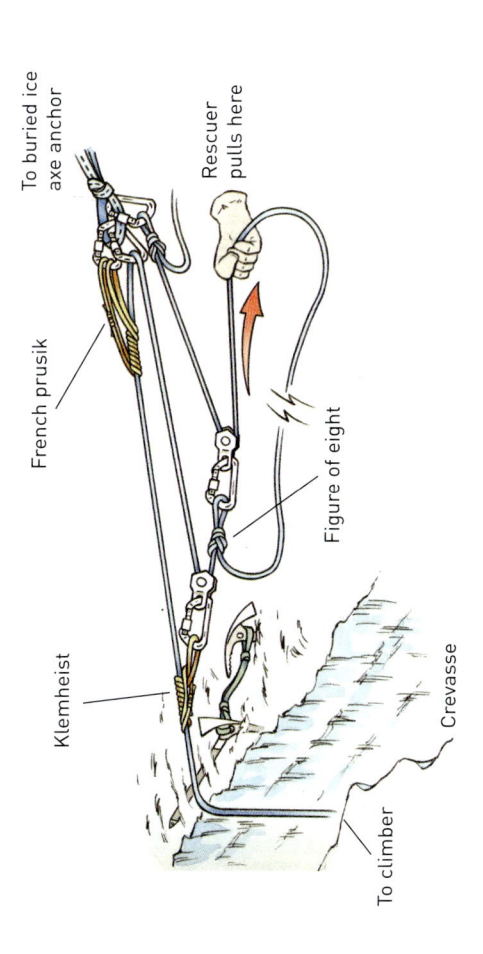

CREVASSE RESCUE

Fig. 57 Improving the hoist to a 6:1 pulley system

- To buried ice axe anchor
- Rescuer pulls here
- French prusik
- Figure of eight
- Klemheist
- To climber
- Crevasse

RESCUE SLEDS

A rescue sled is useful, even if you have called a rescue helicopter, to move the victim a short distance. Unfortunately, making a sled that will stay together and transport a victim is not simple. There are commercially available kits to make sleds, but they weigh 2 or 3kg, and with only a small amount of kit you can make your own sled. This system is definitely crude and does not slide easily, but it does work.

- Clamp the tips of the skis with two pieces of 0.3cm aluminium measuring 2 x 25.5cm, which can be bolted together with a wing nut in the centre and one on either end.
- If you have not got a clamp, tension two krabs (Fig. 58).
- If you have not got an aluminium bar you can use a shovel at the front.
- Brace the bindings of the skis by clamping two collapsible ski poles, an ice axe or a shovel handle. This creates the main frame, which can be strengthened by lashing ski poles length-wise between the bindings and the ski tip. The addition of the poles also helps lift the body of the victim a bit further off the snow.
- Place a bivvy sack on top to create a slippery surface.
- Pad the binding area and poles with an empty rucksack and foam pads.
- Place the victim's head near the ski tips, and use a rope if necessary to tie the victim in place, wrapping it directly around the ski edges if necessary.

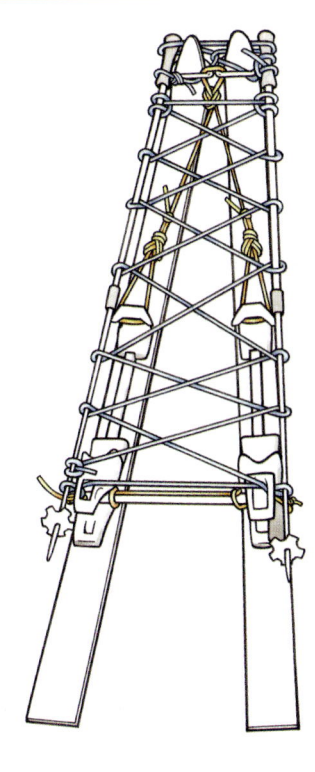

Fig. 58 A self-made rescue sled using skis

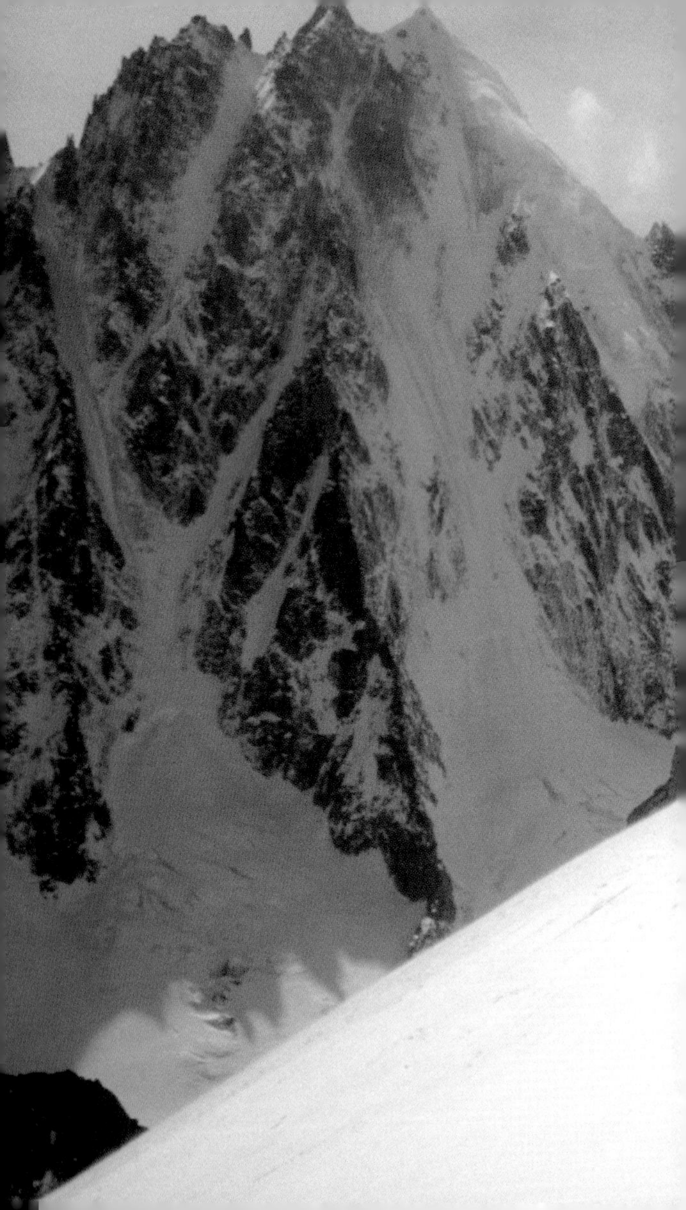

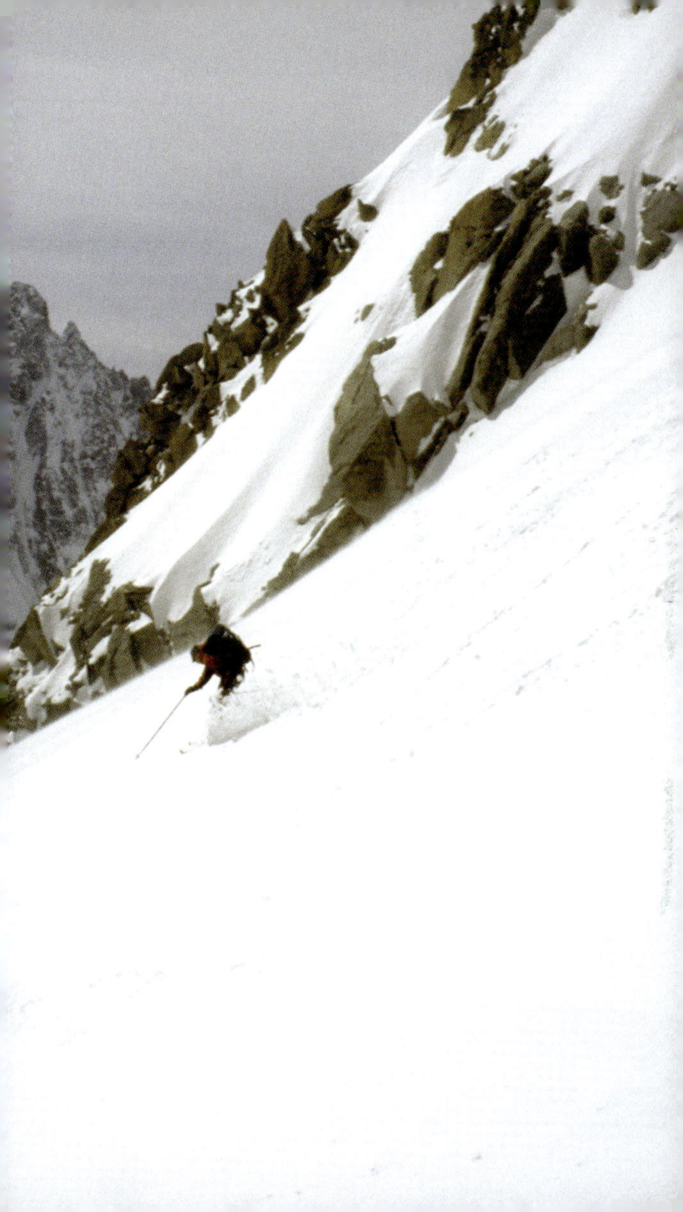

OFF-PISTE SKIING

Only IFMGA guides are qualified to take you ski mountaineering or work off-piste in glacial terrain in the Alps. Some ski instructors are allowed to take groups off-piste too, so long as they don't travel across glaciers, but the tour hosts and reps who commonly show skiers around pisted runs within large resorts are definitely not allowed to go off-piste (check the insurance details of anyone taking you out).

Guides are trained to look after groups off-piste and on glaciers, and also to find the best snow for their clients to give you a great day's skiing. They are, however, not trained as professional ski instructors.

Kate Scott skiing in deep snow, Chamonix, Mont Blanc, France

AVALANCHE DANGER SCALES

NORTH AMERICAN AVALANCHE DANGER SCALE

The following scale is used in the United States and Canada.

Probability and trigger	Degree and distribution of danger	Recommended action in back country
Low (green)	Natural avalanches very unlikely. Human triggered avalanches unlikely. Generally stable snow. Isolated areas of instability.	Travel is generally safe. Normal caution advised.
Moderate (yellow)	Natural avalanches unlikely. Human triggered avalanches possible. Unstable slabs possible on steep terrain.	Use caution in steeper terrain.
Considerable (orange)	Natural avalanches possible. Human triggered avalanches probable. Unstable slabs probable on steep terrain.	Be increasingly cautious in steeper terrain.

AVALANCHE DANGER SCALES

Probability and trigger	Degree and distribution of danger	Recommended action in back country
High (red)	Natural and human triggered avalanches likely. Unstable slabs likely on a variety of aspects and slope angles.	Travel in avalanche terrain is not recommended. Safest travel on windward ridges of lower angle slopes without steeper terrain above.
Extreme (red/black border)	Widespread natural or human triggered avalanches certain. Extremely unstable slabs certain on most aspects and slope angles. Large destructive avalanches possible.	Travel in avalanche terrain should be avoided and confined to low angle terrain well away from avalanche path run-outs.

AVALANCHE DANGER SCALES

EUROPEAN AVALANCHE DANGER SCALE
The following scale is used in Europe.

Degree of hazard	Snowpack stability	Avalanche probability
1 (low)	The snowpack is generally well bonded and stable.	Triggering is possible only with high additional loads on a few very steep extreme slopes. Only a few small natural avalanches (sluffs) possible.
2 (moderate)	The snowpack is moderately well bonded on some steep slopes, otherwise generally well bonded.	Triggering is possible with high additional loads, particularly on the steep slopes indicated in the bulletin. Large natural avalanches not likely.
3 (considerable)	The snowpack is moderately to weakly bonded on many steep slopes.	Triggering is possible, sometimes even with low additional loads. The bulletin may indicate many slopes, which are particularly affected. In certain conditions, medium and occasionally large sized natural avalanches may occur.
4 (high)	The snowpack is weakly bonded in most places.	Triggering is probable even with low additional loads on many steep slopes. In some conditions, frequent medium or large sized natural avalanches are likely.
5 (very high)	The snowpack is generally weakly bonded and largely unstable.	Numerous large natural avalanches are likely, even on moderately steep terrain

APPENDIX

INDEX

ABS Avalanche Airbags 36
abseiling 114–15
alpine touring (AT) 6
altimeters 30
analogue transceivers 26, 28
avalanche danger scale (North American) 127–8
avalanche probes 22, 23
avalanche transceivers 26–9, 36, 62
  searching 51–6, 58
avalanche victims, searching for 51–9
  digging/probing 58–9
  multiple burial search 55, 56–7
  pinpoint search 52, 55
  primary search 52, 53
  secondary search 52, 53–4
  see also avalanche transceivers
avalanches 32–49
  action when caught in 50
  assessing avalanche potential 40
  avoiding 32, 38
  crossing suspect slopes 48–9
  helicopter rescues 60–1
  myths 34
  probes 22, 23
  rescue/survival statistics 33
  route finding 38–49
  searching for victims 51–9
  slope aspect 42
  snowpack tests 43–7
  survival devices 36–7
  survival facts 29
  terrain traps 39
  transceivers 26–9

Black Diamond Avalung 36
burial time 28

climbing skins, see skins
clock (step around) turns 92
clothing 24
compasses 30
corn snow 64
crampons 14, 22
crevasse rescues 108–23
  abseiling to victim 114–15
  action when down a crevasse 109
  hoisting victims 116, 118–21
  rescue sleds 122–3
  ski anchors 110–12
  transferring load to anchors 113
crevasses 103, 106
  prusiking out 116
cross country (Nordic) skiing 4

crust 64

digital transceivers 26, 28
downhill kick turns 90–1
duck walking (*pied en canard*) 15

emergency kits 30
EPIRB (Electronic Position Indicating Beacon) 30
equipment
  altimeters 30
  avalanche probes 22, 23
  avalanche transceivers 26–9, 36, 51–6, 58, 62
  clothing 24
  crampons 14, 22
  emergency kits 30
  GPS (Global Positioning System) 30
  harnesses 24
  harscheisen (ski crampons) 18, 83
  headlamps 30
  ice axes 22, 112
  maps 30, 38
  mobile phones 26, 30, 60, 62
  navigation aids 30
  radios 30
  reducing weight 20
  repair kits 31
  rescue kits 25
  rucksacks 24
  shovels 21, 22
  ski bindings 4, 10–12
  ski boots 4, 9
  ski crampons (harscheisen) 18, 83
  ski mountaineering boots 9
  ski poles 19, 22, 84
  skins 7, 16–17, 76–81
  skis 6–8, 71–3
  snow saws 22, 46
  snowshoes 13–15
  sun protection 30

falling 100–1
  self-arrest technique 101
firn snow 64
flares 30
food 30

goggles 30, 98
GPS (Global Positioning System) 30
granular snow 64

harnesses 24
harscheisen (ski crampons) 18, 83
headlamps 30
helicopter rescues 60–1
hoisting 116, 118–21
  assisted 119
  improving the hoist 121
  simple pull 116
  two-team pull 116

unassisted 120
using pulleys 118–21
hydration 30

ice 64
ice axes 22, 112

loaded column test 46
loading 40

maps 30, 38
mobile phones 26, 30, 60, 62
multiple burial searches 55, 56–7

neve snow 64
Nordic (cross country) skiing 4
North American avalanche danger scale 127–8

off-piste skiing 126

passive tags 28
pied en canard (duck walking) 15
pinpoint searches 52, 55
PLB (Personal Location Beacon) 30
powder 64
primary searches 52, 53

radios 30
repair kits 31
rescue kits 25
rescue sleds 122–3

rescues
avalanche victims: searching for 51–9
helicopter rescues 60–1
see also crevasse rescues
route finding 38–49
assessing avalanche potential 40
avoiding avalanche terrain 38
crossing suspect slopes 48–9
preparations 62
slope aspect 42
snowpack tests 43–7
terrain traps 39
rucksacks 24
Rutschblock test 46–7

secondary searches 52, 53–4
self-arrest technique 101
shovel test 44–5
shovels 21, 22
ski anchors 110–12
ski bindings 4, 10–12
ski boots 4, 9
ski crampons (harscheisen) 18, 83
ski mountaineering boots 9
ski pole test 44
ski poles 19, 22, 84
ski test 45
skiing signals 99

INDEX

skiing techniques 70–3, 98–107
　carrying skis 71–3
　controlling speed in steep terrain 100
　in crevassed terrain 103, 106
　descending roped-up 106, 107
　falling 100–1
　getting back up in deep snow 101
　glaciated terrain 103
　holding a fall 106
　roping up when skinning 104–5
　self-arrest technique 101
skinning 80–9
　descending 84
　on hard snow 81–2
　roping up 104–5
　track setting 86–7
　turning 90–7
　using harscheisen 83
　using poles 84
　see also skins
skins 7, 16–17, 76–81
　attaching 16, 76
　balling up 78
　care of 76, 77
　long-term maintenance 79
　replacing 77
　see also skinning
skis 6–8
　waxing 7
　carrying 71–3

slopes
　altitude and 67
　aspect 42, 66
　estimating angles 68–9
　weak spots 49
smoke flares 30
snow
　finding good snow 66–9
　types of 64
snow saws 22, 46
snowpack
　loading 40
　tests 43–7
snowpack tests 43–7
　loaded column test 46
　Rutschblock test 46–7
　shovel test 44–5
　ski pole test 44
　ski test 44–5
snowshoes 13–15
　bindings 14
　technique 14–15
step around (clock) turns 92
sun protection 30
sunglasses 30
survival devices 36–7

transceivers 26–9, 36, 62
　searching 51–6, 58
turning 90–7
　clock (step around) turns 92
　downhill kick turns 90–1
　uphill kick turns 94–7

MOUNTAIN WALKING AND TREKKING

This book is ideal for novices and experienced walkers alike, as it includes everything you need to know about how to navigate in the mountains. It includes information on weather, and tells you how to prepare for your trek, including packing your rucksack and the equipment you will require. It also demystifies the art of scrambling and tells you how to ascend Via ferrata safely.

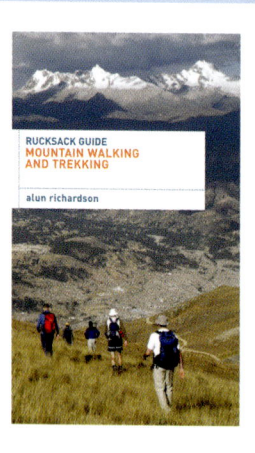

ROCK CLIMBING

Rock climbing can be a tough, sometimes dangerous, physical and mental challenge. This book covers everything you need to know to be safe when ascending steep rock formations, including efficient movement skills.

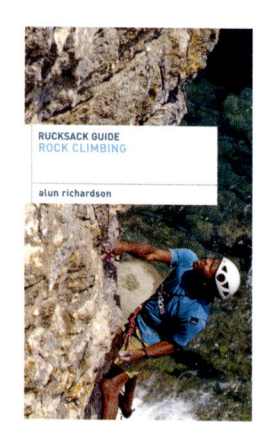

OTHER BOOKS IN THE SERIES

MOUNTAINEERING IN REMOTE AREAS OF THE WORLD

This is the essential handbook for planning and undertaking mountaineering expeditions around the world. It offers concise guidance, including where to go and when, advice on dangerous animals and minimising your impact on the environment, and dealing with extreme situations.

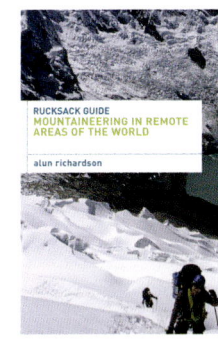

ALPINISM

Venturing to the Alps for the first time can be daunting. This volume covers everything you need to know about ascending these magnificent mountains, in summer and winter.

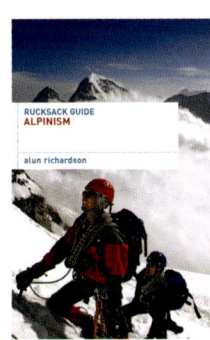

WINTER MOUNTAINEERING

Mountains transformed by snow and ice are a world apart from lush summer slopes. This volume provides you with the techniques to explore wintry plateaus, tackle rocky ridges and ascend snowy slopes.

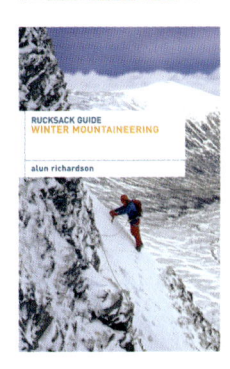

NOTES